IRELAND

IRELAND

BY WILLIAM W. LACE

LUCENT BOOKS
P.O. BOX 289011
SAN DIEGO, CA 92198-9011

Library of Congress Cataloging-in-Publication Data

Lace, William W.
    Ireland / by William W. Lace.
        p.   cm. — (Modern nations of the world)
    Includes bibliographical references and index.
    Summary: Examines the land, people, and history of Ireland and
discusses its current state of affairs and place in the world today.
    ISBN 1-56006-448-X (lib. bdg. : alk. paper)
    1. Ireland—Juvenile literature.   [1. Ireland.]   I. Title.
II. Series.
  DA906.L33   1999
  941.5—DC21   98-55676
                                                              CIP
                                                              AC

Copyright © 1999 by Lucent Books, Inc.
P.O. Box 289011, San Diego, CA 92198-9011
Printed in the U.S.A.

CONTENTS

INTRODUCTION

"A TERRIBLE BEAUTY"

The little Irish village of Pettigo is perched on each side of the placid River Termon, its narrow streets and quaint buildings imparting a picture-postcard charm. The river, however, divides more than just the village. On the western bank, in the Republic of Ireland (Eire), stands a statue dedicated to four villagers who were killed while fighting against the British in 1922. On the eastern bank, in Northern Ireland, is a monument commemorating a British victory.

Pettigo stands as a metaphor for Ireland—outwardly idyllic yet condemned by its past to a deeply divided present. The face of Ireland is one of spectacular beauty and quiet enchantment; its countryside is largely unspoiled, and its people are warm and outgoing. That face, however, masks a centuries-long legacy of conflict, poverty, brutality, and bloodshed.

The latest struggle—pitting Catholics against Protestants in Northern Ireland—is only one of many that have plagued the island since recorded history. When not fighting their British overlords or, before that, the Viking invaders, the Irish have fought among themselves. Their fierce pride and independent spirit, combined with a legendary combativeness, have made elusive the peace and unity they have long sought.

STRUGGLE FOR EXISTENCE

Mere existence has been a struggle for the Irish. Lacking in natural resources, isolated by its location, and dominated throughout most of its history by Great Britain, Ireland has been a land of grinding poverty, with the vast majority of its people living ever close to the edge of disaster. In one case, the potato famine of the 1840s, destitute Irish starved to death by the hundreds of thousands in what was perhaps the greatest natural disaster to hit a European country since the Black Death of the 1300s.

Progress has come slowly to Ireland, which was barely touched by such civilizing, modernizing forces as the Renaissance, the Enlightenment, or the Industrial Revolution.

Although Northern Ireland fared better because of its connection with Great Britain, the Republic of Ireland remained one of the most backward countries in Europe until 1973, when its entry into the European Union accelerated economic growth. The concept of Europe's civilizing influence on Ireland is ironic considering that western European civilization was greatly influenced—even saved from destruction, some say—by the great Irish missionaries, theologians, and educators of the 700s and 800s.

Contributions of Culture and People

Ireland's contributions are by no means confined to those ancient missionaries. Always renowned for gifts of song, dance, and storytelling, the Irish have given the world such literary figures as Oscar Wilde, George Bernard Shaw, and James Joyce; the music of U2; and the phenomenally popular *Riverdance* and *Lord of the Dance* troupes.

Not the least of Ireland's gifts to other nations have been the Irish themselves. To escape the poverty of their homeland, millions of Irish have emigrated over the last two hundred years, mostly to Great Britain, the United States, New Zealand,

Though it is an important member of the modern-day European community, Ireland is still a mostly agrarian and vastly undeveloped country.

*Rock band U2 is just
one of the many Irish
contributions to the
worlds of art and music.*

and Australia, their spirit and energy contributing mightily to those countries. U.S. presidents John F. Kennedy and Ronald Reagan are but two examples of prominent Americans of Irish descent.

It has, indeed, been the spirit of the Irish—their strength, resilience, and humor in the face of adversity—that has enabled them to endure all the burdens heaped on them by nature, foreign invaders, and one another. As the twentieth century drew to a close, the Irish faced perhaps the biggest challenge of all—a chance for unity and peace. Could they break the chains of the past and find a way to live in harmony? Or would Ireland continue in the somber tradition expressed by Irish poet William Butler Yeats?

Now and in time to be,
Wherever green is worn,
All changed, changed utterly:
A terrible beauty is born. [1]

THE LAND

Ireland has been called an offshore island of an offshore island, a description accurate of both its geographical location and its historic position on the edge of European civilization. Ireland sits at the far end of Europe; to its west is the Atlantic Ocean and to its east is the larger island of Britain, which has separated itself physically and culturally from the mainland. Historian J. H. Andrews calls Ireland "a wall flower at the gathering of west-European nations." [2]

The island itself covers 32,589 square miles, making it slightly larger than South Carolina and slightly smaller than Maine. It contains two countries, or rather one country and part of another. The twenty-six counties of the south and far northwest, 85 percent of the land mass, make up the Republic of Ireland. The six counties in the northeast—most of the area historically known as Ulster—compose Northern Ireland, a part of the United Kingdom along with England, Scotland, and Wales.

The island measures 291 miles from north to south and is 171 miles across at the widest point. The eastern shore, facing Britain, is the gentlest, with sandy beaches stretching almost unbroken from Dublin south to Rosslare in County Wexford. Those beaches have furnished easy landings for invaders over the centuries. On the southern shore beaches alternate with rocky headlands, while the western and northern coasts, battered by the Atlantic, are wild and rugged, providing some of the most spectacular scenery in Europe.

Much of the land of Ireland is like the Atlantic coast—beautiful yet inhospitable. The central lowlands, lying two hundred to four hundred feet above sea level, are ringed with highland masses. The granite Caledonian uplands, which cover much of Northern Ireland and the northwest part of the Republic, are an extension of the mountains of highland

9

Scotland. Indeed, Ireland and Scotland are separated at one point by a gap of only thirteen miles.

THE SOUTHERN MOUNTAINS

In the south red sandstone uplands run from the Wicklow Mountains in the southeast westward to Macgillicuddy's Reeks in County Kerry, which boasts Ireland's highest peak, Carrantuohill, at 3,414 feet. The southern mountains are more recent geologically than those in the north and are part of the same formation as the mountains across the Irish Sea

 ## EXILES IN ERIN

The Irish have always been passionately attached to the land. In pre-Christian days most Irish believed that spirits inhabited trees, rocks, and hills. After the coming of the Normans in 1169, however, the Celtic Irish slowly lost control of the land they so loved. By the 1700s most land was owned by British overlords, and the Irish became like servants in their own home.

In 1589 a poet named Ó Gnímh expressed this feeling in his "Exiles in Ireland." This excerpt is from an English translation by Samuel Ferguson in 1834 and is found in *Ireland* by A. R. Orme.

For the plain shall be broke
By the share of the stranger,
And the stone-mason's stroke
Tells the woods of their danger.

The green hills and shore
Be with white keeps [castles] disfigured,
And the Mote of Rathmore
Be the Saxon churl's haggard!

We starve by the board [table],
And we thirst amid wassail—
For the guest is the lord,
And the host is the vassal!

Through woods let us roam,
Through the wastes wild and barren;
We are strangers at home!

in Wales. Most of the good soil has been washed away from the slopes of the glens formed by these rugged peaks, rendering them generally unfit for large-scale farming, although the rough grass and heather make good grazing for sheep and cattle. In parts of the west, most notably the Aran Islands in Galway Bay, the clay soil is so thin and poor that farmers have had to make their own, mixing beach sand and seaweed in order to grow a few vegetables or some grass for grazing.

Between the northern and southern uplands is a broad central area roughly thirty miles on either side of a line from Dublin in the east to Galway in the west. The land here is better but by no means entirely suited to agriculture. Running along the border between Northern Ireland and the Republic is an area of drumlins, small but very steep hills formed by deposits of earth left by melting glaciers ten thousand years ago. To the south much of the land—3 million acres, or one-seventh of Ireland—is covered by peat bogs, decayed plant matter compressed over centuries into a solid form. High in carbon content, peat is still burned to heat many Irish farmhouses and not too long ago was the only source of fuel for most of the Irish.

Jagged, rocky shorelines are typical of Ireland's western shores.

Aside from the highlands, drumlins, and bogs, about 50 percent of the land of Ireland is suitable for productive farming, but much of that is so intermingled with bogs that it makes it difficult at best. In earlier centuries vast stands of oak and birch also limited the amount of arable land; however, so much woodland has been cleared since the mid-1500s that today forests cover less than 5 percent of the land.

THE GIANT'S CAUSEWAY

Two natural geological formations are especially unusual. At the northernmost tip of Northern Ireland, in County Antrim, the Giant's Causeway stretches into the Atlantic from the base of a 395-foot cliff. It is made up of an estimated thirty-seven thousand columns, most of them hexagonal, that fit together in such precision that it is hard to believe it is natural rather than man-made. It was formed about 60 million years ago, when a layer of volcanic basalt cooled and cracked into the column formation.

The Irish, of course, have another version. In their legends the giant Finn MacCool, lonely for his fair lady across the sea on the island of Staffa in Scotland, decided to build a path so that he could visit her and so laid the causeway down. Sure enough, similar columns are found on Staffa.

The other noteworthy natural phenomenon is the Burren, a vast stretch of horizontal limestone slabs in County Clare on the south shore of Galway Bay. The name comes from the Irish word *boireann*, meaning "rocky land." Wind and rain have stripped the topsoil and gouged fissures into the limestone; in these fissures grow a variety of Mediterranean and alpine plants found nowhere else in Ireland. The rocky terrain and high winds make it nearly impossible for trees to grow, and the area has a wild, desolate look. A surveyor, mapping the site for English ruler Oliver Cromwell in the 1640s, called the Burren "a savage land, yielding neither water enough to drown a man, nor tree to hang him, not soil enough to bury him." [3]

Though the precisely sized and fitted rock formations in the Giant's Causeway look like they are man-made, they are a naturally occurring phenomenon.

THE FORESTS REBORN

Before humans arrived in Ireland, the island was almost completely covered by forest. Gradually, the forest was cleared to free up land for crops and pastures. This process was greatly accelerated under the Normans, who needed lumber for the towns they built, and especially in the 1500s as the English won complete control of the island.

By 1930 only about 1 percent of Ireland was forested. Over the last fifty years, however, the government of the Republic has made a determined effort to rebuild the island's forests and to make Ireland a lumber-exporting country. Similar efforts are under way in Northern Ireland.

Most of the "plantations" are conifers—Stika spruce, lodgepole pine, and Norway spruce. Environmental groups have objected, saying that the acidity produced by these trees could harm fish and wildlife. They urge the planting of more hardwoods, such as oak and beech. The bogland soils where the plantations take place, however, are not suitable for hardwoods.

Farmers have been slow to turn to forestry because of the long wait for a monetary return. The Stika spruce, for instance, takes forty years to mature, and it is regarded as one of the faster-growing species. Still, private tree planting rose from 741 acres in the early 1980s to more than 23,000 acres in 1992. The percentage of land covered by forests is now about 5 percent and is expected to rise to 10 percent by the year 2000.

Because of high meat prices established by the European Union, most of the agriculture in Ireland is livestock-based. Both the Republic and Northern Ireland are large exporters of beef, pork, and mutton. Dairy and poultry farming are also widespread, with milk, cheese, and eggs shipped all over Europe. Fishing is also a main source of income, primarily in Northern Ireland. Barley, wheat, and oats are the principal crops, and there are some orchards in the north, but few vegetables are grown. In fact, more than half of Ireland's most famous crop—potatoes—is imported.

MINERAL RESOURCES

Ireland is generally poor in mineral resources. Tin, lead, gold, silver, and copper have been mined for centuries, but the minerals on which heavy industry depend—iron and coal—are found only in small quantities. The only oil and natural gas are from a few offshore wells near the southern coast; the rest must be imported. The most commercially successful minerals today are peat and the sands and gravels used by the building industry.

Ireland's climate, known to geographers as western maritime, can best be described in two words—*cool* and *wet*. It certainly seemed that way to the Romans, who named the island Hibernia—"land of eternal winter." The island receives two kinds of air masses moving off the Atlantic Ocean: moist tropical fronts drifting from the south and moist polar fronts from the north. The interplay of these two fronts makes Irish weather highly changeable. A low, clinging mist or light rain in the morning may give way to sunshine by noon and rain again by sundown. It is not at all unusual to have several brief periods of interspersed rain and sunshine within a few hours.

Rainy days are the rule rather than the exception, and there are only an average of about three to four hours of bright sunshine a day. Half of Ireland can expect rain two days out of every three, and in the far west, where the Atlantic fronts come onshore sometimes in gales with winds reaching ninety to one hundred miles per hour, rain can be expected three days out of every four. As would be expected, relative humidity is high, averaging about 80 percent.

Rain falls with such frequency in Ireland that most people are not fazed by it at all.

The Irish people are so used to the rain that they ignore it. Only the rare downpour will bring out umbrellas, drivers do not seem to slow down appreciably, and rural clotheslines are hung with washing—although it is difficult to see how it will ever dry.

Despite the frequency of rainfall, amounts vary widely. Dublin, in the east, receives about thirty inches per year. Belfast, the capital of Northern Ireland, receives thirty-eight inches. Most of the rainfall in the lowlands is light, providing what the Irish call "a soft day." The story is far different in the mountains and in the west. Glensamole, in the Wicklow Mountains only a few miles south of Dublin, averages fifty-three inches while some areas in the mountains of Kerry in the southwest and County Mayo in the northwest average more than 80 inches.

TEMPERATURES

Neither the tropical nor the polar fronts completely dominate the other. As a result, temperatures do not change dramatically from month to month, and seasons are not as sharply divided as in other parts of the world. Extreme temperatures are rare, with Dublin experiencing an average daily low of only thirty-six degrees Fahrenheit in January and an average daily high of sixty-seven degrees in July. In contrast, Warsaw, Poland, actually on a more southerly latitude, has an average low of twenty-six degrees in January and an average high of seventy-five degrees in July.

Frost is frequent in Ireland, despite the moderate temperatures, but snow is much rarer. At Armagh in Northern Ireland, frost has been recorded in every month except July. Even far to the south, at Cahersiveen in Kerry, only May through September is frost-free. Snow, however, is extremely rare in the south. Even in the north, the ground is seldom covered, except in the mountains. Snow or sleet falls on Dublin an average of twelve days a year but only three days in measurable amounts.

The high amount of rainfall gives rise to numerous streams and rivers that crisscross the island. The Shannon, by far the longest river, originates in the hills just a few miles west of the border and meanders 161 miles south before emptying into the Atlantic below Limerick. Throughout the centuries the Shannon has served as a natural barrier, and the counties west of the river have been those least touched by modernization. Other important rivers are the Liffey, the Nore, the Clare, and the Boyne in the Republic and the Lagan and Bann in Northern Ireland. Many Irish rivers abound with fish, particularly salmon, which is a major export.

Of the thousands of lakes in Ireland, none is as impressive as Lough Neagh, which sits in the center of Northern Ireland with five of the country's six counties radiating from it

Ireland's numerous rivers (the product of heavy rainfall) make it an ideal place for fishing.

IRISH PLACE NAMES

Many towns and villages in Ireland take their names from landmarks. Most are derived from the Celtic or Gaelic words, and some took their names from Viking terms. Here are some of the most common:

Baile (place, land): Any of the more than one hundred towns with the prefix *Bally-*, such as Ballybunion, Ballyquin
Beann (peak): Benbaun, Benburb
Cluain (clearing): Clonmacnoise, Clontarf
Cnoc (hill): Knockboy, Knockaderry
Doire (oakwood): Knockaderry, Londonderry
Druim (ridge): Drumcree, Rathdrum
Fiord (Norse for bay): Waterford, Wexford
Inis (island): Enniskillen, Innishfree
Lo (Norse for meadow near water): Wicklow, Arklow
Ros (grove): Roscommon, Roscrea
Staor (Norse for land): Lienster, Munster
Tulach (mound): Tully, Tullamore

---

like spokes of a wheel. It is the largest lake in the British Isles at 153 square miles. Its marshy banks are a bird-watcher's paradise, and the island's tastiest eels are caught in its waters. Legend recounts that the giant Finn MacCool once picked up a piece of land and hurled it into the Irish Sea. The land became the Isle of Man, and the hole it left became Lough Neagh.

POVERTY OF SPECIES

There are far fewer species of animals and plants in Ireland than in Britain and fewer still than on the European mainland. About nine hundred plant varieties are native to Ireland, as compared with fourteen hundred in Britain and about three thousand in France. Similarly, only 33 percent of the reptiles and amphibians, 48 percent of the mammals, and 85 percent of the land birds found in Britain are also native to Ireland. Of the sixteen species of freshwater fish in Britain, only eight are found in Ireland's rivers and lakes.

Ireland has hares and stoats but no weasels or moles, foxes but no wolves, oak trees but no native beech. There is only one variety of lizard and no snakes at all, the legend being that they were all chased from the island by St. Patrick. The real story is that the snakes, and all the other missing plants

The Irish attribute Ireland's lack of snakes to St. Patrick.

and animals, never got to Ireland in the first place. Both Britain and Ireland were once part of the European land mass. Both were almost entirely covered by glaciers in the last ice age and lost virtually all their life forms. After the glaciers melted in about 8000 B.C., both plants and animals began to migrate into the area from central Europe. Two thousand years later, the rising sea separated Ireland from Britain, thus cutting off the natural migration process. After another thousand years, Britain was also cut off from the mainland, but during that millennium many more species came into Britain that never had a chance to reach Ireland.

It is easy to see how Ireland came by its nickname of the Emerald Isle. Even though the island does not have as great a variety of plants as its larger neighbor, its grasslands are much more luxuriant because of the high humidity and constant rainfall. Consequently, most of the pastureland, especially in the south in the spring and summer, is incredibly lush and green—a green that almost leaps out when one approaches the island by air. Likewise, mosses and lichen seem to grow on everything.

A RURAL LANDSCAPE

Ireland is essentially rural, with a population density of 157 people per square mile as compared with 957 in England and 585 in Germany. In fact, the island is far more rural than the statistics indicate. Of the estimated combined population of the Republic and Northern Ireland of 5,129,000, 36.6 percent—well over a third—live in the four metropolitan areas of Dublin, Belfast, Londonderry, and Cork. The rest of the landscape is made up of long stretches of small family farms with an occasional small town or village.

Dublin is the only truly metropolitan city. With a population of 1.2 million, it is four times larger than Belfast, the Northern Ireland capital, and nine times larger than Cork, its nearest rival in the Republic. While Dublin is far more cosmopolitan than other Irish cities, dominating culture, politics, and business, it still retains an Irish flavor, unlike some European capitals that seem to have a completely different character from the rest of the country. The reason is that Dublin has, indeed, remained essentially Irish, unaffected by the immigration that has so marked, for instance, London.

Despite the scattered population, getting around in Ireland is neither quick nor easy, and driving can be frustrating. There are less than two hundred miles of what would be called freeways in the United States, all of them in the Belfast and Dublin areas. The rest of the roadways, although well marked, are often so narrow that one must partially pull over on a grassy shoulder to allow a truck coming the other way to pass by. The better-paved surfaces are generally found in the north, and the main roads there often bypass villages. In the south, however, the roads run straight through villages, where driving is made even more difficult by parked cars taking up half a roadway.

EARLIEST ACCOUNTS

One of the earliest references to Ireland was by the Roman historian Tacitus, who wrote about 100 A.D. that the emperor Agricola "saw that Ireland . . . conveniently situated for the ports of Gaul might prove a valuable acquisition." He added that, "I have often heard Agricola declare that a single legion, with a moderate band of auxiliaries, would be enough to finish the conquest of Ireland."

The Romans never attempted to conquer Ireland, though. Had they tried, Agricola might have found himself the first of many generals to underestimate the Irish. Tacitus's quotations are found in *The Oxford History of Ireland*.

The earliest known appearance of Ireland on a map is that drawn by the Greek geographer Ptolemy, also in about 100 A.D. Names on the map are remarkably accurate, given that Ptolemy never visited either Britain or Ireland and probably got his information second– or thirdhand from sailors and traders.

Ptolemy's map correctly gave the name and position of both the Boyne and Shannon Rivers. He also identified a tribe in Ulster as the Robogdii, which is probably the Dál Riata, also known as the Scotii, the same tribe that later invaded northern Britain and gave its name to the kingdom of Scotland.

The city of Dublin is one of the few major urban centers in a country full of small, rural villages.

Although Ireland has a comprehensive bus network and a less extensive railway system, the best way to see the island is by car. A surprise may be waiting around every turn—a breathtaking view of a mountain or glen, a herd of cattle crossing the road, a thatched-roof cottage, or a ruined castle. Ireland is a lovely land, and if it takes a while to get from one part of it to another, so much the better.

THE PEOPLE

Despite the momentous events of the last century—independence at last from Great Britain, entry into the European Union, and the strides toward modernization—the Irish remain absorbed in their past, a past that has shaped their society. Like the Jews, the Irish have reacted to centuries of oppression by forging a strong national identity. Those who emigrate, and even those generations removed from Ireland, have close ties to their ancestral homeland. St. Patrick's Day, for instance, is celebrated much more in the United States than in Ireland.

Three major factors have shaped the Irish people. The first is their geographic location—an island far from the mainstream of European civilization. Second is the fact that the Celts of Ireland—unlike their British neighbors—had roughly a thousand years in which no major invasions or ethnic additions occurred, a millennium in which a distinctively Irish society was developed. The third has been Ireland's five-hundred-year-long domination by Britain, centuries mostly of poverty and oppression.

Although humans arrived in Ireland much later than in most of Europe, the Celts were by no means the first to reach the island. No record exists of any inhabitation before the Ice Age, and most experts think the first bands of Mesolithic, or middle Stone Age, people arrived about 6000 B.C., around the same time that Ireland was separated from Britain. The land bridge from Scotland may still have been available to them, or they may have crossed over in coracles, small boats made of animal skins stretched over a wooden frame.

These Mesolithic people were nomads, hunting and fishing in areas along the coast. They practiced no agriculture and lived in semipermanent camps as they followed game. They were confined mostly to the northeast, depending on the supply of flint found along the beaches for their tools and weapons.

THE NEOLITHIC PEOPLE

Three thousand years later a new people, the Neolithic, began to replace the old. Their tools, although still stone, were larger and more advanced. With these tools they began to change the face of Ireland by clearing forests to plant crops,

THE CELTS

Around 500 B.C. a people known as the Celts began to arrive in Ireland from Europe. The Celts were composed of many tribes having a common language and culture. They originated in modern-day Austria and eventually spread to Gaul (modern-day France), Spain, northern Italy, Britain, and Ireland.

The Roman general and later emperor Julius Caesar fought several wars against the Gauls, as did his successors. This description of the Celtic tribesmen, which would have applied to the Celts of Ireland as well, was written by Greek historian Diodorus Siculus in the first century A.D. It is found in *A Short History of Ireland* by John O'Beirne Ranelagh.

> Physically the Gauls are terrifying in appearance with deep-sounding and very harsh voices. In conversation they use few words and speak in riddles. . . . They are boasters and threateners and given to bombastic self-dramatization, and yet they are quick of mind with good natural ability for learning. . . . When the armies are drawn up in battle array they are wont [likely] to advance before the battle-line and to challenge the bravest of their opponents to single combat, at the same time brandishing before them their arms so as to terrify their foe. And when someone accepts their challenge to battle, they loudly recite the deeds of valour of their ancestors and proclaim their own valorous quality, at the same time abusing and making little of their opponent and generally attempting to rob him beforehand of his fighting spirit. They cut off the heads of their enemies slain in battle and attach them to the necks of their horses . . . and they nail up these first fruits [the heads] upon their houses.

Celtic warriors conquered and settled most of Ireland in the early sixth century B.C.

mainly wheat and barley. They raised livestock, including pigs, oxen, and sheep. As farmers they were tied to the land, living in permanent settlements, usually self-sufficient farmsteads rather than villages.

Few traces of Neolithic settlements remain, but their magnificent megalithic, or "large stone," tombs can be seen throughout Ireland. Their various tomb styles reveal that they arrived on the island at different times and from different places in Britain or Europe. Earlier tombs consisted of long barrows or galleries, found mostly in the northwest, that housed collective burials and cremations. Single burials were marked by dolmens, stone tripods with capstones. Later arrivals, probably originally from Spain, built large, elaborately carved passage graves, so-called because of the long passages leading to burial chambers. Ornaments found in passage graves show how much more advanced the Neolithic civilization was than the Mesolithic.

In about 1800 B.C. the Bronze Age reached Ireland. Immigrants known as the Beaker People used native copper and imported tin to fashion tools and weapons of bronze. Ireland was becoming more populated, and the competition for good land led to warfare between tribes. The new technology was used to make halberds, spears, and swords. Ireland was growing wealthier as well. Metalsmiths made golden ornaments of such quality that they were exported to Britain and the mainland.

Tribal warfare led to a need for secure dwelling places, and farming families began to enclose their homes with wooden palisades made of timber. Others built crannogs, artificial islands along the shores of lakes on which houses were built and surrounded with high wooden fences. Crannogs were still in use in some remote parts of the island as late as the 1600s.

THE CELTIC CONQUEST

By 500 B.C. a group of people arrived that was to form the basis of Irish society—the Celts. The Celts had originated in modern-day Austria. In around 2000 B.C., they began a pattern of conquest that eventually led to their domination of northern Europe from Ireland and Spain in the west to the shores of the Black Sea in the east. The Celts were tall and warlike, and most had the red hair that became an Irish trademark. They brought with them weapons and tools of iron. These innovations, along with their superior military organization and tactics, including horse-drawn chariots, quickly made them masters of the island.

Livestock raising was the chief occupation of the Celts, who measured wealth in terms of cattle and whose wars usually involved cattle raids. The basic unit of Celtic society was the *fine*, or family group that included all relations in the male line. The *fine* shared wealth, and all members were responsible for the misdeeds of one another. The *fine* worked land in common, and its members lived together in crannogs or other fortified sites. The Celts, however, were exclusively rural. Villages and towns were unknown.

Groups of *fine* made up a *tuath*, or petty kingdom, although the families within a *tuath* might not be related by blood. At one time there were more than 150 of these *tuatha*. The *tuath* was governed by a *rí*, or king, elected by all free men of the *tuath*. Groups of *tuatha* were ruled by a *ruiri*, or great king, who in turn owed obedience to a *rí ruirech*, or king of overkings. The *rí ruirech* ruled a considerable area. Over the centuries the island was divided into five overkingdoms: Munster in the southwest, Lienster in the southeast, Meath in the east, Connacht in the west, and Ulster in the north. In theory, there was also an *árd rí*, or high king, a title claimed by whoever controlled the Hill of Tara, just northwest of present-day Dublin. Despite all of the various kingships, there was no true king of all Ireland for more than a thousand years after the coming of the Celts, and the over kingdoms were constantly at war with one another.

THE GAELIC LANGUAGE

The Celts also brought to Ireland their own language, Gaelic, similar to Celtic dialects spoken in Wales, Brittany, and Scotland. Gaelic developed into the dominant language of the people and is still in everyday use in a few remote regions. The only written language was the Ogham alphabet, a system of carved lines so cumbersome that its use was confined mainly to tombstones.

Instead of depending on a written language, the Celts relied on an oral tradition. The laws were memorized by *brehons*, judges who passed them to succeeding generations, and history was the province of poets and storytellers. Consequently, early Irish history is such a mixture of myth and reality that it is sometimes impossible to separate the two. Such Celtic legends as Finn MacCool and the mighty warrior Cuchulainn may have been based partly on fact. The feats of Naill of the Nine Hostages seem like those of the Greek Hercules, but most scholars agree that there was such a person; for centuries his descendants, the Uí Néill (O'Neal), provided some of Ireland's strongest kings.

Not all the songs and stories carried from farm to farm by wandering bards were about heroes, though. The Celts practiced a form of nature worship in which all things, living and inanimate, had spirits. Magic, mysticism, and the supernatural played large roles in Celtic life, and belief in fairies, the female spirits known as banshees, and the "little people" called leprechauns persisted well beyond the advent of

THE *BÓAIRE'S* PROPERTY

The Celts were divided into several classes, both slave and free. The higher grade of free men were the *bóaires*. This description of a *bóaire's* household, written in the early Christian era, is found in *The Course of Irish History*, edited by T. W. Moody and F. X. Martin.

All the furniture in his house is in its proper place—a cauldron with its spit and handles, a vat in which a measure of ale may be brewed, a cauldron for everyday use, small vessels: iron pots and kneading trough and wooden mugs, so that he has no need to borrow them. . . . He is a man of three snouts: the snout of a rooting boar that cleaves dishonour in every season, the snout of a flitch [piece] of bacon on the hook, the snout of a plough under the ground; so that he is capable of receiving a king or a bishop or a scholar or a *brehon* [judge] from the road, prepared for the arrival of any guest-company. He owns seven houses: a kiln, a barn, a mill . . . a house of twenty-seven feet, an outhouse of seventeen feet, a pig-stye, a pen for calves, a sheep pen. He has twenty cows, two bulls, six oxen, twenty pigs, twenty sheep, four domestic boars, two sows, a saddlehorse, an enamelled bridle, sixteen bushes of seed in the ground. He has a bronze cauldron in which there is room for a boar. He possesses a green in which there are always sheep without having to change pasture. He and his wife have four suits of clothes.

Christianity. Indeed, some elderly farmers remember when one could supposedly curse a neighbor's crops by burying a cow's foot in his potato field.

The Christianizing of Ireland began in 431 A.D., when Pope Celestine authorized the sending of a priest named Palladius to "the Irish believing in Christ."[4] Most of the credit for converting the Irish, however, is given to St. Patrick. According to his own writing, Patrick was born in Roman Britain, captured by Irish raiders, and spent seven years in Ireland as a slave. He escaped, returned to Britain, became a priest, and eventually was sent back to Ireland as a missionary. The exact dates of St. Patrick's mission have been disputed, and some experts think he has been credited with both his work in Ireland from 459 to 490 and that of Palladius from 432 to 461.

St. Patrick is credited with converting the Irish to Christianity and introducing monasticism.

ST. PATRICK'S MINISTRY

Regardless of when Patrick's mission occurred, it left a tremendous impression on Ireland. He worked mainly in the north and west and, in his own words, "baptized thousands," "ordained clerics [priests] everywhere," "gave presents to kings," and "lived in daily expectation of murder, treachery, or captivity."[5] More than two dozen Irish churches trace their founding to Patrick.

Patrick organized the Irish church on the European model in which priests were grouped into dioceses governed by bishops, who in turn were governed by an archbishop. He also, however, introduced monasticism—the banding together of monks or nuns into communities of work, prayer, and study. Monasticism appealed much more to Celtic mysticism, and within a generation of Patrick's death, monasteries like Armagh, Clonmacnoise, and Glendalough were the dominant feature of the Irish church.

During the next two hundred years, from about 550 to 750, Irish monasteries were among the most outstanding centers of learning in Europe. As Germanic invaders such as the Anglo-Saxons in Britain threatened to extinguish Christianity in western Europe, it

PATRICK'S VISION

The man generally credited with converting Ireland to Christianity is St. Patrick. Born into a well-to-do family in Roman Britain, Patrick was kidnapped as a youth by Irish raiders and enslaved. He managed to escape back to Britain and became a priest.

In his *Confession*, this excerpt from which is found in *The Course of Irish History* by T. W. Moody and F. X. Martin, Patrick describes the vision that led him to return to Ireland as a missionary.

And there I saw in the night the vision of a man whose name was Victorious, coming as it were from Ireland, with countless letters. And he gave me one of them and I read the opening words of the letter which were "The voice of the Irish" and as I read the beginning of the letter I thought that at the same moment I heard their voice—they were those beside the Wood of Foclut which is near the Western Sea—and thus did they cry out as with one mouth: "we ask thee, boy, come and walk among us once more."

was kept alive largely through missionaries from Ireland. In Iona, Scotland, St. Columba (ca. 521–597) founded a monastery that, together with its offshoot at Lindisfarne on the eastern coast of England, converted all of northern Britain. St. Columban (ca. 543–615) established Luxeuil in France and Bobbio in Italy. Other Irish monks founded monasteries in Belgium, Switzerland, Austria, and Germany, many of which became centers of learning and civilization.

These two centuries are usually called the golden age of Ireland. Learning and literature were the finest in Europe. The church was the main outlet for artistic expression, and the surviving golden crosses and chalices show a strong blending of Celtic and Latin styles. The Irish church also produced some of the finest illustrations known, including the richly detailed Book of Kells, begun at Iona in the late 700s.

A WARLIKE PEOPLE

Christianity, however, did little to tame the fighting spirit of the Celts, and one warrior of Ulster could say:

I swear by that by which my people swear, since I took spear in my hand I have never been without slaying a

The monastery at Clonmacnoise was built in the time of St. Patrick.

Connachtman every day and plundering by fire every night, and I have never slept without a Connachtman's head beneath my knee. [6]

Indeed, the Irish had no one but one another to fight for a thousand years, neither the Romans nor the Germanic tribes having reached the island. This freedom from invasion came to an end in 795, when strange ships with high curved prows and square painted sails landed near Lambay on the eastern coast and discharged crews of fierce warriors who plundered monasteries and slaughtered the monks. These were the Vikings, and they would battle the Celts for control of Ireland for the next two hundred years.

Vikings is the term used to describe the raiders from the Scandinavian lands. Those in Ireland were mostly from Norway. Their historic reputation as pirates is misleading. Their mission was not mere plunder but to scout lands for possible colonization. This colonization began in Ireland with two fortified settlements on the east coast in 841, one of which, at the mouth of the River Liffey, later became known by the Celtic name of *dubh-linn,* meaning "dark pool." From Dublin and other sites, the Vikings raided the interior, plundering the monasteries.

Colonization slowed after the defeat of a Viking fleet by an O'Neal king in 867. New fleets began arriving in 915, however, and the next few years saw the founding of Waterford, Wexford, Limerick, and Cork. The next century was one of constant warfare with the Vikings raiding inland from their towns on the coast. Significantly, however, their areas of settlement were only around the towns, not in the interior, and they never settled in numbers large enough to have a major impact on the ethnic makeup of the population, as they did across the Irish Sea in England.

Why then, if the Vikings were not all that numerous, were the Irish not able to drive them back into the sea? The answer is that the Irish were, as usual, too divided. Instead of joining against a common enemy, Irish kings allied with Vikings to battle one another.

The Vikings arrived in Ireland in the ninth century. The Vikings founded the city of Dublin in addition to many other settlements.

BRIAN BORU

In the 960s the obscure kingdom of Dál Cais in Munster began to expand under the leadership of its king, Mathgamain. When Mathgamain was killed in 976, his brother, Brian Boru, took the throne. At last Ireland had found its leader. In 999 he defeated the king of Lienster and the Dublin Vikings at the battle of Glen Máma. Three years later, Maelsechlainn, heir of the O'Neal dynasty, surrendered to him without a fight at Tara. Brian became the first king of all Ireland.

Ireland, however, was still Ireland, and Brian was constantly having to deal with pockets of rebellion. In 1014 the ruler of Lienster once more joined with the Vikings, but they were defeated at the battle of Clontarf. It was a costly victory, as described in a Viking saga:

> Swordblades rang on Ireland's coast,
> Metal yelled as shield it sought,
> Spear-points in the well-armed host.
> I heard sword-blows many more;
> Sigurd fell in battle's blast,
> From his wounds there sprang hot gore.
> Brian fell, but won at last. [7]

After their defeat at Clontarf, the Vikings were never again a major force in Ireland. Brian Boru's death, however, brought an end to any kind of unity among the Irish. For the next 150 years the rulers of Munster, Lienster, Connacht, and Ulster (Meath had been absorbed by Munster and Lienster) fought against one another in a series of shifting alliances.

One such conflict was to have momentous consequences. In 1152 the wife of Tiernan O'Ruark, king of Breifne, was

Brian Boru, the first king of a united Ireland, was killed while fighting a Viking army in the battle of Clontarf.

abducted (with her help and consent) by Dermot MacMurrough, king of Lienster. O'Ruark soon got his wife back, but he never forgave MacMurrough. Fourteen years later, after his kingdom was overrun by O'Ruark, MacMurrough fled Ireland looking for help. He sailed to Bristol in England and then to France, hoping to enlist the aid of King Henry II of England.

The kings of England at this time were English in name only. They were the Norman-French descendants of William the Conqueror, duke of Normandy, who had successfully invaded England in 1066. They had vast holdings in France, spoke French rather than English, and had never made any attempt to expand their conquest to Ireland.

THE LETTER OF HENRY II

Henry listened with interest to MacMurrough. In 1155 Pope Adrian IV, disturbed by stories of scandals within the Irish church, had issued a decree giving Henry the authority to invade, reform, and rule Ireland. Henry had been far too busy with wars in France, but now he saw an opportunity. He could not come in person, he said, but he gave MacMurrough a letter authorizing his nobles in England, Wales, and France to come to the Irishman's aid.

In May 1169 an Anglo-Norman force landed at Bannow Bay and marched on the city of Wexford. The Vikings of Wexford marched to meet them, expecting to encounter another brave but lightly armed band of Irishmen. Instead, they found ranks of foot soldiers and archers flanked by armed knights on huge warhorses. The Vikings were driven back into Wexford and surrendered the city the next day. The long entanglement of Ireland and England had begun.

The newcomers were mostly from the hills of Wales and had a long history of fighting the native population there. Chief among them was Richard de Clare, earl of Pembroke, nicknamed "Strongbow" by the Irish. He won a series of victories, culminating in the summer of 1171 when the English, after having been trapped inside the walls of Dublin by an army of Irish and Vikings, slipped out of the city at night and surprised their enemies at Castleknock. The victory established the English as the dominant military force in Ireland.

Henry II was alarmed by the success of Strongbow, who he feared might establish his own kingdom in Ireland. He crossed the Irish Sea, landing at Waterford with a large army

King Henry II of England was the first monarch to involve the English in the affairs of Ireland.

and marching north. Everyone—English, Irish, and Vikings—acknowledged his supremacy. He made Strongbow earl of Lienster, and other English lords were made earls in Munster, Meath, and Ulster. In 1174 Roderic or Rory O'Connor was recognized by Henry as high king of the unconquered parts of the island, and it seemed as if peace might come to Ireland.

ENGLISH EXPANSION

Henry, however, soon was busy in France again, and the English took advantage of his inattention to seize more land from the Irish. Their tactic was to march into an area and build a wooden fortress that they later replaced with a stone castle. From these enormous castles, the remains of which dot the island, they ruled the surrounding countryside. By 1250 three-fourths of Ireland was ruled by the English.

Ireland was prosperous and peaceful under English rule. The only warfare was along the border of the unconquered lands. The English introduced advanced methods of agriculture, common law and trial by jury, a representative parliament, and a system of administration still in place though much modified. More important, they brought Ireland closer to European civilization, and education and literature flourished.

In the second half of the 1200s, however, the English conquest began to falter. Rather than coming to Ireland in greater numbers, soldiers returned to England to fight in wars in Scotland and—during the Hundred Years' War (1337–1453)—in France. Many settlers fled back to England during the Black Plague in 1348–1350. The Irish chieftains grew stronger and increasingly found allies within the ranks of the English lords, many of whom had married into Irish families and were, in the words of one frustrated English official, "more Irish than the Irish themselves."[8]

The English government in Dublin tried to regain control in 1366 by forcing through Parliament the Statutes of Kilkenny, which attempted to keep the English and Irish apart, forbidding intermarriage and the speaking of Gaelic and wearing of

Irish-style clothing by English nobles. The measure failed, and by 1450 England controlled only the area around Dublin known as the Pale, from which comes the expression "beyond the Pale," meaning barbaric.

WARS OF THE ROSES

Outside the Pale, Ireland was ruled by two great families: the Butler earls of Ormond and the Fitzgerald earls of Desmond and Kildare. When the Wars of the Roses broke out in England between the York and Lancaster branches of the ruling Plantagenet family, the Butlers supported the Lancastrians and the Fitzgeralds the Yorkists. In 1462 the Butlers were defeated by the earl of Desmond at Piltdown. Later, however, Desmond

STRONGBOW

The man who led the Anglo-Norman conquest of Ireland was Richard de Clare, earl of Pembroke, who was nicknamed "Strongbow." This description of him by a contemporary historian, Gerald of Wales, is found in *The Course of Irish History*, edited by T .W. Moody and F. X. Martin.

> He had reddish hair and freckles, grey eyes, a feminine face, a weak voice and a short neck, though in almost all other respects he was of a tall build. He was a generous and easy-going man. What he could not accomplish by deed he settled by the persuasiveness of his words. . . . When he took up his position in the midst of battle, he stood firm as an immovable standard round which his men could regroup and take refuge. In war he remained steadfast and reliable in good fortune and bad alike. In adversity no feelings of despair caused him to waver, while lack of self restraint did not make him run amok when successful.

Strongbow is buried in Christ Church Cathedral in Dublin, which he began building in 1172. An effigy of an armored knight marks the spot, but it is not the effigy of Strongbow. The original was destroyed in 1562 when part of the roof collapsed. Since the tomb was referred to in many contracts as the spot where money was to be exchanged, another effigy had to be found so that the payments could continue. Another effigy—portraying a member of the FitzOsbert family from Drogheda—was installed. A fragment of the original figure can be seen next to it.

was executed for treason, and his brother-in-law Thomas Fitzgerald, earl of Kildare, became the most powerful man in Ireland.

Thomas was created governor of Ireland by the Yorkist king Edward IV, and the Kildare title passed in 1478 to his son, Gerald More Fitzgerald, known as "the Great Earl," who maintained power even when Henry VII (Tudor), a Lancastrian, became king of England. Kildare, however, became involved in a plot to put a York back on the throne, and Henry decided that, for the safety of his throne, he had to reassert the power of England over Ireland. He sent a deputy, Sir Edward Poynings, to Dublin in 1494 to force through Parliament a measure known as Poynings's Law. Like the Statutes of Kilkenny, it tried to halt the spread of Irish culture among the English. More important, however, it provided that the Irish Parliament could meet only with the king of England's permission and then only pass laws that had been approved in advance.

The Great Earl's power was curbed by Poynings's Law, but he obeyed, as did his son, Gerald Oge, who succeeded him in

The conflict between Catholics and Protestants in Ireland has its roots in King Henry VIII's break from the Catholic Church in 1533.

1513. In 1533, however, the Kildares had a new reason for opposition to England. Henry VII's son, Henry VIII, broke with the Roman Catholic Church and had himself proclaimed head of the Church of England. Kildare opposed the change in religion, and Henry, fearing he might side with England's Catholic enemies, called him to London. On June 11, 1534, Kildare's son Thomas, called "Silken Thomas" because of the silk fringe on the jackets of his followers, rode into St. Mary's Abbey in Dublin, flung down his symbols of authority, and declared Ireland in revolt against England.

THE FALL OF SILKEN THOMAS

The revolt of Silken Thomas was crushed without mercy. Under Sir William Skeffington, an English army battered down the walls of Maynooth Castle, the Fitzgerald stronghold, and executed all who survived the assault. Thomas himself was executed in 1537, and

IRELAND AND ENGLAND

From the first landing of the Anglo-Normans in Ireland in 1169 to the present-day "Troubles" in Northern Ireland, the Irish have conflicted with their British neighbors. Over the centuries, as the Irish have rebelled time and again, the British have deplored what they considered an ungovernable people.

In 1868 British philosopher John Stuart Mill, then a member of Parliament, published an essay in which he claimed that the fault lay not with Irish barbarism but with British ignorance and arrogance. Mill's quotation is found in *A Short History of Ireland* by John O'Beirne Ranelagh.

> The difficulty of governing Ireland lies entirely in our own minds; it is an incapability of understanding. . . . [The British point to] a special taint in the Irish character, but . . . there is probably no other nation of the civilized world, which, if the task of governing Ireland had happened to devolve on it, would not have shown itself more capable of that work than England has hitherto done. The reasons are these: first, there is no other nation that is so conceited of its institutions and of all its modes of public action, as England is; and secondly, there is no other civilized nation which is so far apart from Ireland in the character of its history, or so unlike it in the whole constitution of its social economy; and none, therefore, which if it applies to Ireland the modes of thinking and maxims of government which have grown up within itself, is so certain to go wrong.

the power of the Kildares was broken. For the next four hundred years Ireland would be ruled by an English governor and there would be an English army in Dublin.

The final conquest by the English would bring about the completion of the ethnic makeup of Ireland. Henry VIII's daughters, Queens Mary I and Elizabeth I, began a process of "plantation"—the forced displacement of Irish by English colonists. The English settlers brought into Leix and Offaly in the 1550s and into Munster in the 1580s were the last significant group to join the Celts, Vikings, and Anglo-Normans. There would be an extensive plantation into Ulster from Scotland in the early 1600s, but the newcomers—although Protestants in a Catholic land—were of the same basic Celtic stock as the Irish.

Queen Elizabeth I encouraged English settlers to colonize Ireland in the late-sixteenth century.

Thus, Ireland has remained basically a Celtic country through the ages. The Celts were so firmly established between 250 B.C. and the Viking invasions that they were able to absorb not only the Vikings but also the Normans and the English. After the English conquest, Ireland's poverty would make it a place for people to leave rather than one attracting new people. As a result, the population of Ireland today is remarkably homogenous. Of the approximately 5 million people in both the Republic and Northern Ireland, the overwhelming majority are of Celtic-Irish descent with probably fewer than fifty-thousand Jews, Indians, Muslims, and Chinese.

Although homogeneous as a people, the Irish have remained disunited in politics and religion. The tragedy of the English conquest was that it was incomplete. Had the kings of England been less interested in chasing dreams of glory in France, they might have finished the task of unifying the British Isles begun by William the Conqueror. Their indifference, however, resulted in an island on which the majority of the people—who are poor and Catholic—have lived in close contact with and were under the heel of the rich Protestant minority. The sparks from the clash of these two Irelands have ignited the fires of conflict that continue to burn.

ENGLAND-IRELAND;
PROTESTANT-CATHOLIC

The English conquest of Ireland, which began with the first Anglo-Norman landing in 1169, was finished by the Tudors some four hundred years later. For the first time since Brian Boru, the island was unified under a single ruler, but it was a foreign ruler with a foreign religion. The result would be a permanent state of conflict between Protestant and Catholic, a conflict that would eventually split the island in half.

The Tudor conquest was neither quick nor easy. Three major rebellions occurred, each one of which was crushed and each one of which diminished the power of the Irish and Anglo-Irish nobles. The last and most serious, by Hugh O'Neill, earl of Tyrone, was broken by his defeat and the surrender of his Spanish allies at Kinsale in 1601. Tyrone fought a lone guerrilla war for two more years but finally submitted on March 30, 1603. He and his fellow nobles received pardons from England's new king, James I, but were unwilling to remain ordinary subjects in a land where they had been virtual kings. In 1607 Tyrone, along with his brother-in-law Rory O'Donnell, earl of Tyrconnel, and more than ninety other Irish nobles went into voluntary exile in France. This "flight of the earls" brought the ancient Celtic lordships to an end, left the Irish leaderless, and paved the way for perhaps the most significant event in the history of Ireland—the plantation of Ulster.

Plantations, the displacement of native Irish with settlers from England, had been tried before—in Leix and Offaly in the 1550s and in Munster in the 1580s—but with too few colonists to be successful. In contrast, the plantation of Ulster was well organized and well financed. Planters, the wealthy individuals and companies who received grants of land from one to two thousand acres, brought thousands of families into what had been Ireland's most remote region. Some of the newcomers were English, but most were from

THE MUNSTER REBELLION

The history of the British in Ireland is one of constant rebellion followed by ruthless reprisals, and the reprisals fill a storehouse of bitter Irish memories. To the Irish, such incidents are more than history. Events centuries ago are just as alive in their memory as those that happened in their parents' time.

Such events took place in the 1500s when the long rebellion of the FitzGerald family in Munster was finally crushed by the forces of Queen Elizabeth I of England. One of her commanders, Sir Humphrey Gilbert, freely wrote to the queen about

> putting man, woman and child to the sword. . . . I keep them from their harvest, and have taken great preys [prize] of cattle from them, by which it seemeth the poor people . . . offer themselves with their wives and children rather to be slain by the army than to suffer the famine that now in extremity beginnith to pinch them.

Famine did, indeed, pinch the people of Munster. The poet Edmund Spenser, serving as a secretary to the English government in Ireland in the 1580s, described the countryside:

> Out of every corner of the woods and glens they came creeping forth upon their hands, for their legs would not bear them. They looked like anatomies of death; they spake like ghosts crying out of their graves; they did eat of the dead carrions, happy were they if they could find them, yea, and one after another soon after, insomuch as the very carcasses they spared not to scrape out of their graves. And if they found a plot of watercresses or shamrocks, they flocked there as if to a feast.

Both quotations are found in *A Short History of Ireland* by John O'Beirne Ranelagh.

---

the lowlands of Scotland—solemn, industrious Presbyterian farmers who quickly laid out neat farms, established market towns with local industries, and built churches and schools.

NEW CITIES

To serve the needs of the settlers, new cities like Belfast and Bangor were built and older ones like Derry and Armagh were restored and expanded. Derry lay in the section of Ulster planted by a group of merchants from London, so when it was rebuilt it was also renamed—Londonderry.

Large sections of land were seized for plantation to keep the Protestant newcomers segregated from the Irish. As had happened with earlier efforts, however, there were not enough settlers. Many native Irish were needed as tenant farmers and laborers, so they stayed in the plantation areas but in the worst economic conditions and on the worst land. There were enough settlers, however, to make the plantation a success. The newcomers flourished while the Catholic Irish among them sunk deeper into poverty. As geographer A. R. Orme wrote, "The seeds of Ireland's present political division were sown and fertilized in the seventeenth century."[9]

The next crisis occurred in the 1640s, when England was torn by a conflict between King Charles I and his Puritan Parliament. In Ireland Catholics planned a massive revolt in 1641. They claimed to support the king but actually wanted to try to break free of England. Although a drunken conspirator accidentally spoiled the plot to seize government buildings in

While Irish Catholics publicly supported King Charles I during England's civil war, their true aim was revolution and a break from England.

Dublin, the rebels succeeded in gaining control over most of Ulster; on several occasions Protestant settlers were massacred by Catholic troops.

When the English civil war ended with the execution of Charles I, Oliver Cromwell, now ruling England as "lord protector," led an army to Ireland. His battle-hardened troops swept away any Irish resistance, showing no mercy to the defeated Catholics. When the city of Drogheda, a few miles north of Dublin, held out against him, he battered it into submission with artillery and then massacred all the inhabitants, soldiers and civilians alike. The city of Wexford suffered the same fate. Throughout Ireland hundreds of thousands died, and Cromwell became a symbol of English oppression that has endured throughout the centuries. "To us," a modern-day Irishman says, "he is like Hitler." [10]

THE CROMWELLIAN SETTLEMENT

Cromwell's mission, however, was one of conquest as well as of revenge. He had promised land to the officers and soldiers who had helped him defeat Charles I, and he looked to Ireland as the place to find it. The so-called Cromwellian Settlement divided Catholic landowners into two categories. Those who had taken part in the rebellion lost their lands, and many emigrated to France, as had the earls a half-century earlier. Those who could show that they had not been rebels were allowed to own land, but not the same land. Their ancestral holdings, often the best land in Ireland, were confiscated and they were forced to accept often poorer property west of the River Shannon in Connacht and Clare. In 1641 Catholics had owned 59 percent of the land in Ireland. A survey in 1688 showed that their share had dropped to 22 percent.

Unlike the plantation of Ulster, the Cromwellian Settlement did not have much effect on the ordinary Irishman working the land. Instead, the poor tenant farmer exchanged a Catholic landlord for a Protestant one. "What it created," writes historian Adian Clarke, "was not a Protestant community but a Protestant upper class." [11]

More trouble lay ahead for the Catholics of Ireland. The English monarchy was restored in 1660 by Charles II, who was succeeded in 1685 by his brother, James II, a Catholic. When the new king began to favor Catholics, his English subjects rebelled, fearing a general return to Catholicism. Leading English nobles invited James's son-in-law, the Protestant William of Orange, to invade the country from the Netherlands. William invaded, a good part of James's army went over to him, and James fled to France.

WAR OF THE TWO KINGS

The French king, Louis XIV, wanted to bring England under his control and loaned James money and weapons with which to try to regain his kingdom. In addition, James was counting on help from the Catholics of Ireland. He landed at Kinsale in March 1689 and, to secure the allegiance of the Irish, promised to reverse the Cromwellian Settlement.

The resulting conflict is known in Irish as the *Cogach an dá rí,* or "War of the Two Kings." France sent seven thousand troops to help James, but he could not gain control of Protestant Ulster and William landed there in 1690 with a force made up of English, Dutch, German, and French Protestant soldiers. The two armies met on July 12 at the River Boyne, about twenty-five miles north of Dublin. After a fierce battle, during which William was slightly wounded, James and his army retreated to the south.

When Oliver Cromwell and his Puritan forces achieved victory in the English civil war, they turned their attention to the conquest of Ireland.

Although the war dragged on another year, finally ending with the surrender of the French at Limerick on October 3, 1691, the battle of the Boyne became, for Irish Protestants, what the Fourth of July is to Americans. It marked the beginning of a long process by which to be Protestant in Ireland—especially in Northern Ireland—was to be considered superior. The battle's anniversary is celebrated today in Northern Ireland with Protestant parades, often punctuated by bloody clashes with Catholics.

William was fairly lenient with the rebels, allowing more than fourteen thousand to emigrate to France. Known as "the wild geese," they would continue to fight for Catholic causes in various European armies. Many of the remaining Catholic landowners were dispossessed for having supported James, and the amount of Ireland owned by Catholics

The ascendancy of the Protestants in Ireland, particularly in the north, began with William of Orange's victory over England's Catholic king, James II, at the battle of the Boyne.

fell to 14 percent. The revenge of the Protestants was not in taking away the Catholics' land, however, but in stripping them of their rights through a series of measures known as the Penal Laws.

THE PENAL LAWS

Enacted by the Protestant-dominated Parliament between 1695 and 1709, the Penal Laws prohibited Catholics from sitting in Parliament or even from voting in parliamentary elections. Catholics could not attend universities, practice law, become officers in the army or navy, teach school, or even own a horse worth more than five pounds. Even more important, the laws worked to prevent Catholics from buying or inheriting land. By the middle of the 1700s, the portion of land owned by Catholics fell to 7 percent.

The Protestant philosopher Edmund Burke called the Penal Laws

a machine of wise and elaborate contrivance and as well-fitted for the oppression, impoverishment, and degradation of a people, and the debasement in them of human nature itself, as ever proceeded from the perverted ingenuity of man.[12]

A CLERGYMAN CONVERTED

After the defeat of the forces of Catholic king James II by those of Protestant king William III in 1690–1691, a series of measures known as the Penal Laws was passed that strove to keep the Catholic majority in a permanent state of servitude. Catholics were banned from all important professions and from serving in the government.

The Penal Laws also attempted to limit the freedom of Catholics to worship. The Registration Act of 1704 required every Catholic priest to register with the government and to take an oath of allegiance to the British crown.

Many priests refused to register and held services outdoors in defiance of the laws. Others, however, not only registered but also converted to Protestantism, much to the dismay of their families and friends. This song from 1739, found in *The Course of Irish History*, edited by T. W. Moody and F. X. Martin, was said to have been composed by the mother of a clergyman in Donegal.

Woe to you, Dominick O'Donnell,
Alas for anyone who ever saw you;
On Sunday you were a priest
And on Monday morning a minister.
Come back, come back, love,
Come back, love, and do not leave me;
Come back my share of the world,
For unless you come back you'll not see the eternal glory.
You abandoned Peter and Paul,
You abandoned John and their kindred,
You abandoned the queen of the universe
Though it is she who is constantly praying for us.

Indeed, the object of the Penal Laws was not to convert the Catholics but to keep them as an underclass of poor laborers and tenant farmers.

William's victory and the Penal Laws ushered in what is known as the Protestant Ascendancy. Landlords grew fabulously wealthy at the expense of their tenants. Some lived in luxury in England while others built fabulous country houses. Not all Protestants, however, were ascendant. The established church was the Anglican Church, or Church of Ireland, which viewed the Ulster Presbyterians with almost as much distaste as they did Catholics. The Test Act of 1704 made membership in the Church of Ireland a requirement for holding government office, and Presbyterian farmers in the north suffered from some of the same abuses—evictions and increased rents—as their Catholic counterparts in the south. Secret societies were formed to oppose these abuses—the Catholic Whiteboys (so-called because they wore white shirts over their clothing) in the south and the Protestant Hearts of Oak and Hearts of Steel in Ulster. Such groups terrorized landowners and were the forerunners of the private armies that have plagued Ireland ever since.

THE UNITED IRISHMEN

In addition, the government of Great Britain (England having united with Scotland in 1704 to form the United Kingdom) enacted laws that protected British farmers and businessmen at the expense of Ireland, both Protestant and Catholic. As a result, Protestants and Catholics began to find they had a common cause. In 1791 a young lawyer named Theobald Wolfe Tone founded the United Irishmen movement, which contained both Catholics and Presbyterians and worked to establish Ireland as an independent republic.

In the meantime Great Britain had modified the Penal Laws. Revolutions in America (1776) and in France (1789) had raised fears of a similar uprising in Ireland. Led by Henry Flood and Henry Grattan, the Irish Parliament sought and won repeal of the part of Poynings's Law that prohibited it from originating legislation. In 1793 Catholics were given the vote and the right to hold public office, except in Parliament.

The lifting of the laws against Catholics, however, was too much for the Protestants of Ulster, where competition for

CROPPIES

During the 1798 rebellion of the United Irishmen, British troops were given free rein to torture and punish anyone suspected of being a rebel. Especially singled out were those Irishmen who had cut, or cropped, their hair short in an imitation of the Republicans of the French Revolution of 1789.

These men were derisively called croppies and were subjected to a form of punishment called the pitch-cap. A paper cap filled with molten tar was jammed down on a victim's head, allowed to adhere, then set on fire. The only way the victim could remove it was to tear it off along with most of his hair and portions of his scalp.

The name also gave rise to a popular song sung by the Protestants of Ulster. It was titled "Croppies Lie Down," and this excerpt is from *The Green Flag* by Robert Kee.

> Oh, Croppies ye'd better be quiet and still
> Ye shan't have your liberty, do what ye will,
> As long as salt water is found in the deep
> Our foot on the neck of the Croppy we'll keep.
> Remember the steel of Sir Phelim O'Neill
> Who slaughtered our fathers in Catholic zeal
> And down, down, Croppies, lie down . . .

land had led to violence between the Protestant Peep o' Day Boys (so-called because of their dawn attacks on Catholic farms) and the Catholic Defenders. In 1795 the Peep o' Day Boys and similar groups joined to form the Orange Order, named for William of Orange and dedicated to the suppression of Catholics in Ulster.

Faced with such opposition, the British government failed to complete the repeal of the Penal Laws. Frustrated, the United Irishmen turned to France for help, a country that was currently at war with Britain. French emperor Napoléon Bonaparte, however, was too occupied elsewhere to send more than a small force that landed at Killala in the northwest in August 1798. It was joined by many Irishmen but was surrounded and surrendered on September 8. The next month a small expedition sailed from France to Ireland but was defeated in a sea battle. Tone, serving as an officer aboard the French flagship, was captured and committed suicide.

THE ACT OF UNION

The 1798 rebellion brought the problem of Ireland to the forefront of British politics. Prime Minister William Pitt decided that the best way to achieve peace in Ireland was to make it part of Great Britain; likewise, Irish representatives would participate in London's Parliament rather than having separate parliaments. Despite opposition in both Great Britain and Ireland, Pitt succeeded and the 1801 Act of Union made Ireland a part of the United Kingdom.

The union failed to satisfy Irish Catholics. Many of the Penal Laws had been repealed, but Catholics still could not sit in Parliament or hold higher positions in the government or armed forces. Leading the fight for full rights was a young lawyer named Daniel O'Connell. In 1823 O'Connell formed the Catholic Association, which soon had thousands of members from all levels of society.

O'Connell directly challenged the laws by running for Parliament in 1828. He was overwhelmingly elected, 2,057 votes to 982 for his landowner opponent, and the British government had a problem. If they denied O'Connell his seat, the Catholic Association might stage riots. While neither the duke of Wellington (the prime minister) nor his chief minister, Sir Robert Peel, favored Catholic emancipation, many within their ruling Conservative Party did, so on April 13, 1829, all restrictions on Catholics were lifted.

O'Connell's next cause was nothing less than the repeal of the Act of Union and the restoration of the Irish Parliament. His tactic was to convene huge gatherings of supporters—"monster meetings"—to force the British to meet his demands. At one meeting in 1843, at the fabled Hill of Tara, more than one million people attended. Impressive as they may have been, the monster meetings failed to achieve their purpose. Peel, now prime minister, was against repeal and had the support of his party. The government banned a huge meeting planned for Clontarf, site of Brian Boru's great victory, and when O'Connell complied, the repeal movement lost its momentum.

YOUNG IRELAND

The repeal movement, however, had one lasting consequence. A group of young radicals formed a new organization, Young Ireland, which preached that all the Irish, whatever their religion or class, should band together and seek complete separation from Britain—by constitutional means if possible or, if not, by force. Young Ireland was not well organized, and a rebellion in 1848 was easily put down and most of the leaders jailed. Its ideas, however, would be picked up by others and would become the core of later movements.

Politics were not Ireland's only concern in the 1840s. A general prosperity had resulted in a dramatic growth in population—from 5 million in 1800 to 8 million in 1841. Since most

Daniel O'Connell formed the Catholic Association to fight discrimination against the Irish and to repeal the Act of Union, which had made Ireland part of Great Britain.

THE GREAT FAMINE

During the potato blight of the late 1840s, the resulting famine caused more than 1 million deaths in Ireland. Another million, faced with starvation, emigrated, many to the United States. In the 1850 census 25 percent of the population of New York City had been born in Ireland.

The situation was made worse by the failure of England to do much to relieve the suffering of the Irish. The prevalent economic theory of the time was one of allowing nature to take its course. Also, the extent of the tragedy was neither known nor appreciated in England. Indeed, Prime Minister Robert Peel at first attributed stories of mass starvation to what he called an Irish tendency to exaggerate.

It was therefore with a feeling of surprise and shock that a *New York Times* reporter landed in Ireland at the height of the famine. This excerpt from his account was published in the Irish journal *Muintir Acla*.

Across in a field a death-white corpse is being flung into a mass grave—his skin stretched over protruding bones. I note this horrifying image in my note book. I ask myself why is this tragedy passing unnoticed to the outside world? Where is the help? Two miles onwards I enter a cottage or, more so, a glorified hovel. On entering, the overpowering stench of death and fever fills my nostrils and leaves a sickening sense in my stomach. A smouldering fire is in the hearth. Over in the corner a mother clutches to her child. Her eyes are red from crying. She does not know of our presence in the cottage. I go over and, to my horror, find that the child is dead.

This I now realise the mother knows and clutches to her baby. The baby is obviously dead for a couple of days. I flee from the cottage—the image of the dead child being intolerable to look at. I walk briskly back to my carriage and tell my driver to drive as fast as he can to the ship departing for America. I cannot wait in this death-filled country a minute longer.

When a fungus decimated the potato crop in the mid-nineteenth century, more than 1 million Irish starved to death.

agricultural products were sold abroad by landlords, the vast majority of people had come to depend on the potato as their main source of food. In August 1845, after a particularly wet summer, a fungus called *Phytophthora infestans* attacked and ruined most of the potato crop for the next four years. The result was a major disaster. The population of Ireland fell by about 2 million persons. One million emigrated, many to America. Another million starved to death.

Tragically, agricultural production remained high, but most of the crops other than potatoes were sold abroad by landlords instead of being used to relieve the suffering of the Irish. Also, the prevailing economic philosophy in Britain at the time was that government should interfere in economic affairs as little as possible. Consequently, Britain did little to help the Irish. Some English leaders even said the Irish had brought the disaster on themselves. In addition to the horrible loss of life, the Great Famine, as it came to be known, also created a lasting bitterness in the Irish toward Britain.

The horrors of the famine only fueled the arguments of those who wanted a complete separation from Britain. A new organization, the Irish Republican Brotherhood, or the Fenians, was formed in 1858. The Fenians differed from Young Ireland in that they thought force was the only way to throw off the British yoke. Although they were quickly put down when they mounted an uprising in 1867, their ideas persisted.

The spirit shown by the Fenians and other groups convinced British prime minister William Gladstone to try to correct some of the injustices done to the Irish. Under his Church Act of 1869 the Church of Ireland was no longer the official church and Protestants and Catholics were equal—at least in the eyes of the law.

THE LAND LEAGUE

Religion, however, was only part of the problem. The majority of the people still lived as poor tenants, and they were growing poorer as landlords raised rents. In 1879 the Irish Land League was formed by Michael Davitt, a working-class Catholic, and Charles Stewart Parnell, a Protestant landowner. Their struggle, known as "the Land War," took place on two fronts. In Ireland, Davitt organized demonstrations against landlords who evicted tenants and provided aid to the destitute families. Most effective of all, landlords found themselves unable to get workers or to sell their products locally.

Arthur Griffith, an Irish politician, advocated a return to home rule for Ireland.

This tactic, when applied to one landlord, Charles Boycott, added a new word to the English language.

In London, meanwhile, Parnell and the other Irish representatives were able to bring Parliament to a virtual standstill by stalling every piece of legislation. Finally, convinced that the old system would no longer work, Gladstone's Liberal Party government passed a series of bills that gradually reduced the power of the landlords and allowed tenants to own land.

Gladstone was also convinced that the ultimate solution to the Irish problem was to grant "home rule," establishing an Irish parliament that, while still subordinate to Britain's Parliament, would govern Irish affairs. He introduced home-rule bills in 1886 and 1893, but both were defeated because of opposition from the Conservative Party in the House of Commons and from the House of Lords.

Despite such efforts, the desire for separation from Britain grew. It was demonstrated in the Gaelic revival that began with the formation in 1884 of the Gaelic Athletic Association, which was dedicated to preserving traditional Irish sports. In 1893 the Gaelic League promoted a return to the Irish language. In 1908 Sinn Féin (Ourselves Alone) was founded by Irish political leader Arthur Griffith, who said that Ireland should return to its status under the Act of Union—a separate country with a separate parliament but still under the British crown. The Fenians were revived and continued preaching the establishment of an independent republic through violent revolution.

The desire for separation was not universal, though. The Protestants of Ulster feared that either home rule or a republic would leave them a vulnerable minority. When it appeared in 1912 that a home-rule bill would be passed, they took action. Crying "Home rule is Rome rule," lawyer Edward Carson convinced thousands to sign the Ulster Covenant, promising any action—including violence—to prevent separation. A secret army, the Ulster Volunteer Force, was organized. In answer, Catholics in Dublin founded the Irish Volunteers in 1913, but just when it appeared civil war was inevitable, World War I broke out and the entire home-rule question was shelved.

The question of separation, however, did not go away. In 1916, hoping to take advantage of Britain's commitment to the war in France, the Fenians and other radicals, led by Patrick Henry Pearse, launched a rebellion on April 24, the Monday after Easter. They seized the Dublin post office and some other government buildings. Fighting in the streets lasted a week. Only about 1,000 men took part, however, and

THE EASTER RISING

The rebellion in 1916 known as the Easter Rising did not have the support of most of the Irish people. It was quickly put down by police and British troops and might have been a relatively minor event had it not been for the events that followed.

The British, determined to make an example of the rebels, executed sixteen men. One of them, James Connolly, had been badly wounded and had to be tied in a chair in front of the firing squad. The brutality of the executions aroused anger among the Irish and a great deal of sympathy in England, and the sixteen men became martyrs for the cause of freedom and heroes in the eyes of the people.

The last to be executed was Roger Casement. His speech, given during his trial, is found in *A Short History of Ireland* by John O'Beirne Ranelagh.

> If true religion rests on love, it is equally true that loyalty rests on love. The law I am charged under has no parentage in love, and claims the allegiance of today on the ignorance and blindness of the past. . . . Loyalty is a sentiment, not a law. It rests on love, not restraint. The government of Ireland by England rests on restraint, and not on law; and since it demands no love it can evoke no loyalty. . . . For if English authority be omnipotent—a power, as Mr. Gladstone [the British prime minister] phrased it, that reaches to the very ends of the earth—Irish hope exceeds the dimensions of that power, excels its authority, and renews with each generation the claims of the last. The cause that begets this indominatable persistency, the faculty of preserving through centuries of misery the remembrance of lost liberty—this surely is the noblest cause ever man strove for, ever lived for, ever died for.

the rebels were forced to surrender to British troops. About 380 people had been killed; more than half of these were civilians caught in the crossfire.

The importance of the Easter Rising lay in its failure. Ninety rebels were sentenced to death, and sixteen were eventually executed despite a wave of protests. The executions deepened hostility in Ireland toward Britain. As a result the country, except for Ulster, moved solidly behind Sinn Féin, now led by Griffith and Eamon De Valera, who had been a rebel leader during the uprising. In the election of 1918, Sinn Féin won 73 of Ireland's 105 parliamentary seats. Instead of going to London, however, the Sinn Féin members proclaimed a republic and set up their own body, the Dáil Éirann, or Irish Assembly, with De Valera at its head. To protect the new government from British retribution, the Fenians under Michael Collins organized a new force, the Irish Republican Army (IRA).

War broke out early in 1919 between the IRA and British troops, who needed auxiliary policemen because so many Irish policemen had resigned. These auxiliaries, many of whom were former British soldiers who had served in World War I, were called the "black and tans" because of the black belts and holsters they wore over their khaki uniforms. The conflict was an ugly one, marked by terrorism, assassinations, and the murdering of civilians and burning of their homes.

Eventually public opinion in Britain and America forced the British government to back down. The 1920 Government of Ireland Act divided the island into two self-governing areas, north and south, each with its own parliament. Then, in December 1921, after months of negotiation, a treaty was signed that made the twenty-six counties in the south a British dominion—the same status enjoyed by Canada and Australia—called the Irish Free State. Ulster, meanwhile, elected to remain part of Great Britain, although with its own parliament.

CIVIL WAR

Although such Sinn Féin leaders as Griffith and Collins had signed the treaty, radicals who wanted a completely independent republic violently opposed it. In January 1922 the Dáil voted narrowly, sixty-four to fifty-seven, to accept the treaty; however, the Republicans launched a new war, during which Collins was killed in an ambush. At last, in May 1923, the Republicans were defeated and something like peace finally was achieved.

The Irish Free State still was technically ruled by the king of Great Britain, and the British maintained two naval bases. In 1932, however, De Valera, who had opposed the treaty, won control of the Dáil. His party, Fianna Fáil, or Soldiers of Destiny, promised a new constitution that would make the

Michael Collins founded the Irish Republican Army, the military arm of the Sinn Féin political party.

Eamon De Valera advocated a complete break from England.

Irish Free State into a completely independent republic. The constitution was approved in 1937, and the British withdrew their naval bases the next year. It was not until 1949, however, that the country formally declared itself the Republic of Ireland (officially Eire) and was so recognized by Britain.

After centuries of struggle the southern counties of Ireland had achieved independence, but the Republic still was among the poorest of European nations. Northern Ireland, as the six counties of Ulster were officially known, enjoyed more prosperity, but the prosperity was one-sided. The best land and the best jobs went to the Protestant majority, while their Catholic neighbors grew poorer and more bitter. The situation was one almost guaranteed to explode into violence, and the explosion would come in the mid-1960s with the start of "the Troubles," the latest and still unfinished chapter in the tragedy of Irish history.

THE TROUBLES

The year 1968 was marked by revolutionary fervor around the world. Soviet tanks were sent to crush a rebellion in Czechoslovakia. A shocked United States watched on television as demonstrators battled police at the Democratic Party convention in Chicago. And, in Northern Ireland, tension between Protestants and Catholics boiled over into what the Irish, with characteristic understatement, called "the Troubles." This unrest would turn into more than three decades of bloody civil war threatened—and still threatens—to tear the region asunder.

The repression of Catholics began almost as soon as the six counties of Ulster decided to remain part of Great Britain in 1921. Catholics were promised that boundaries would be redrawn so that many areas would become part of the Republic of Ireland. In the end, only a few minor changes were made, trapping the Catholics in a hostile country. Most refused to take part in the new government of Northern Ireland, preferring to hope for the eventual unification of the island. In so doing, the Catholics established themselves, in Protestant eyes, as enemies of the state.

The Protestants feared unification just as much as the Catholics prayed for it. Consequently, everything possible was done to prevent Catholics from gaining any power. When public housing became available, most of it was given to Protestants, and only homeowners could vote in local elections. Government was firmly in the hands of the Ulster Unionist Party, leaders of which were invariably members of the militantly Protestant Orange Order. Similar discrimination existed in employment, and the Royal Ulster Constabulary (RUC) and the volunteer Special Constables, charged with keeping law and order, were heavily Protestant.

THE ULSTER COVENANT

Much of the groundwork for the Troubles was laid in the late 1800s and early 1900s; during this time some of the leaders of Great Britain, weary of the constant problems of trying to govern Ireland, wished to allow Ireland to govern herself. The movement was known as "home rule" and would have allowed the Irish their own parliament to run their own internal affairs while foreign affairs would still be in the hands of Britain.

The prospect of home rule was violently opposed by the Protestants of Ulster. They formed the majority in Ulster but feared that home rule would make them a minority in an all-Ireland parliament. When, in 1912, it appeared that home rule might be approved by the British Parliament, Sir Edward Carson urged Ulster's Protestants to sign a "solemn league and covenant." On September 28, 1912, he and more than four hundred thousand Unionists signed this agreement, found in *A Short History of Ireland* by John O'Beirne Ranelagh.

> Being convinced in our conscience that home rule would be disastrous to the material well-being of Ulster as well as to the whole of Ireland, subversive of our civil and religious freedom, destructive of our citizenship and perilous to the unity of the Empire, we whose names are underwritten, men of Ulster, loyal subjects of His Gracious Majesty King George V, humbly relying on the God whom our fathers in days of stress and trial confidently trusted, do hereby pledge ourselves in solemn covenant throughout this our time of threatened calamity to stand by one another in defending for ourselves and our children our cherished position of equal citizenship in the United Kingdom and in using all means which may be found necessary to defeat the present conspiracy to set up a Home Rule Parliament in Ireland. And in the event of such a Parliament being forced upon us, we further solemnly and mutually pledge ourselves to refuse to recognize its authority.

"All means which may be found necessary" clearly included armed violence. In January 1913 Carson helped establish the Ulster Volunteer Force, a paramilitary organization still active in Northern Ireland.

Catholics were slow to organize against such discrimination. It was not until 1967 that the Northern Ireland Civil Rights Association (NICRA) was formed, modeling itself closely after civil rights groups in the United States. In fact, the group's first anthem was "We Shall Overcome"; eventually the movement's official anthem was changed to "A Nation Once Again."

THE FIRST MARCH

In June 1968 an eighteen-year-old woman—the secretary of a Unionist (Protestant) politician and engaged to a policeman—was awarded a house even though some Catholic families had been on the waiting list ten years or more. In protest, Catholics engaged in sit-ins in vacant houses and were roughly evicted by the RUC. The result was the first protest march, held in Dungannon on August 24. This march was peaceful, but the time of peace was almost at an end.

A second march was held on October 5, this one in Londonderry. By now Protestant politicians had become alarmed and were determined to take action. As the marchers moved into Duke Street, they found their way barred by ranks of RUC police. At the same time, more policemen moved in behind them. As protest leaders Gerry Fitt and Eamon McCann tried to make

NORTHERN IRELAND

Atlantic Ocean

Rathlin Island

Portrush

North Channel

Coleraine

ANTRIM

Londonderry

Carnlough

LONDONDERRY

R. Bann

R. Main

Ballymena

Larne

R. Foyle

Bangor

Lough Neagh

Belfast

TYRONE

Lisburn

Lough Erne

R. Lagan

DOWN

FERMANAGH

Enniskillen

Armagh

Downpatrick

Upper L. Erne

ARMAGH

Newcastle

Newry

Irish Sea

speeches, the police charged from both sides. Marchers, including women and children, were clubbed to the ground. Some marchers broke through to Craigovon Bridge only to be driven back by water cannons.

That night Bogside, the Catholic section of Londonderry, erupted in riots. Police cars were stoned and set on fire with gasoline bombs. Windows of shops owned by Protestants were shattered. The Troubles had begun.

A few days later a group of radical students at Queens University in Belfast founded the People's Democracy. Among them was Bernadette Devlin, a fiery twenty-year-old who would become the youngest woman ever elected to Britain's Parliament and one of the most eloquent spokespersons for Catholics. Over the next few months, the People's Democracy took control of the Catholic movement. Soon, the focus went from one of civil rights to complete freedom from Britain. "They weren't really interested in civil rights," says historian Conor O'Brien. "They were interested in revolution." [13]

A policeman fires tear gas at rioters in Londonderry, Northern Ireland, in 1969.

REVEREND IAN PAISLEY

On the other side of the political-religious fence, the Protestant Unionists let it be known that they considered any concessions to the Catholics as treason and as steps that would lead to a unified Ireland dominated by the Catholic Church. Their leader was the Reverend Ian Paisley, who was just as radical a Protestant as Devlin and the People's Democracy leaders were radical Catholics. A charismatic leader and brilliant orator, Paisley vowed to use any means—including violence—to keep Protestants in power. When Catholics planned marches, Paisley planned simultaneous countermarches, knowing he could count on the RUC and Special Constables for help if violence broke out.

Thus, Northern Ireland began to polarize. Those advocating a middle ground—both Protestants and Catholics—were branded as traitors. Terrence O'Neill, prime minister of Northern Ireland, tried to bring peace by enacting a series of reforms that would, among other things, end housing discrimination.

THE SOUTHERN VIEW OF PARTITION

When the Unionists, as those who wanted to remain part of Great Britain were called, objected strenuously to the concept of home rule for Ireland, some politicians began to put forth the idea that the island would be divided—home rule applying to the south but not to the north.

When John Redmond, leader of the Irish Party (the principal group in the south advocating home rule), indicated he might be willing to accept partition on a temporary basis, a storm of protest arose. As might have been expected, Catholic nationalists were opposed since partition would isolate Catholics in the north. Yet, the Protestant Unionists in the south also objected since partition would put them in a minority.

In 1914, when the Home Rule Bill finally became law, the *Irish Times*, a Unionist newspaper in Dublin, carried an editorial against partition. This excerpt is found in *The Green Flag* by Robert Kee.

> [Unionists were] patriotic Irishmen and intended to live in their country unless and until they were driven out by intolerable misgovernment. . . . [But] if we are to have self-government, Ireland must be a self-governing unit. That instinct is implanted deeply in the heart of every thoughtful Irishman, Unionist or Nationalist. In the first place the country is too small to be divided between two systems of government. In the next place, the political, social and economic qualities of North and South complement one another; one without the other must be miserably incomplete. For Southern Unionists . . . the idea of the dismemberment of Ireland is hateful. . . . In a word, the permanent partition of our country is inconceivable.

Catholics said his efforts were not enough; Protestants said they were too much. He resigned six months later.

By the time O'Neill resigned, the situation had moved from one of confrontation to open warfare. On January 4, 1969, a peace march from Belfast to Londonderry was attacked at Burntollet Bridge by a club-wielding mob. As Bernadette Devlin recalls,

> From lanes at each side of the road a curtain of bricks and boulders and bottles brought the march to a halt.

The Reverend Ian Paisley, a militant Protestant, has long vowed to fight to keep Catholics from making political gains in Northern Ireland.

From the lanes burst hordes of screaming people wielding planks of wood, bottles, laths, iron bars, crowbars, cudgels [clubs] studded with nails, and they waded into the march beating hell out of everybody.[14]

O'Neill was succeeded by James Chichester-Clark, but the violence continued to increase. On July 16 police chasing a group of rock-throwing youths broke into the wrong house by mistake. Without pausing to check, they clubbed everyone in sight, including the owner, a forty-two-year-old taxi driver named Samuel Devenney, who later died, the first victim of the Troubles.

BRITISH TROOPS ARRIVE

On August 12 a Protestant parade attempted to force its way into Bogside. The residents forced them to retreat under a hail of stones, bricks, and gasoline bombs. More than a thousand people were injured, and the British government sent in regular army troops to try to bring order.

At first the Catholics welcomed the British soldiers almost as liberators. That changed in the summer of 1970, when five people were killed and seventy-five injured when the army stormed into the Catholic-held "no-go" sections of Belfast and the "Free Derry" section of Londonderry to search for weapons. This confirmed in many Catholic minds that their only source of protection was the Irish Republican Army, specifically the Provisional IRA, or Provos, which had split from the regular IRA in 1969.

The IRA went on the offensive in 1971 with a series of bombings in which several British soldiers were killed. The British government reacted with a program of internment, arresting and imprisoning suspected IRA terrorists without formal charges or trials. Internment targeted only Catholics, who were frequently tortured while in prison.

Internment served only to increase the violence. On January 30, 1972, British troops fired into a crowd of marchers in Londonderry, killing thirteen people in what came to be called Bloody Sunday. The IRA retaliated by bombing the Aldershot military barracks in February, killing seven people.

By now it was clear to Britain that the government of Northern Ireland was incapable of dealing with the situation. On March 24 Stormont—the Northern Ireland Parliament—was abolished and direct rule from London was instituted. The battle lines were now drawn for more than twenty years of violence—the IRA on one side and the British army, RUC, and private Protestant armies such as the Ulster Volunteer Force on the other.

THE EXECUTIVE COMMITTEE

As the bombings and murders continued, efforts were made to achieve peace. In 1973 the British negotiated a settlement in which Northern Ireland would be governed by a power-sharing executive committee made up of both the Unionist Party and the Social Democrat and Labor Party (SDLP), a

"A NATION ONCE AGAIN"

One of the most influential men in Irish history was Thomas Davis, a leader of the Young Ireland movement in the 1840s. He founded Ireland's first weekly newspaper, the *Nation*, in 1842 and used it to advocate separation from Great Britain.

When the civil rights movement in Northern Ireland began in 1967, it first borrowed the anthem "We Shall Overcome" from the American civil rights movement. Later, however, leaders of those mostly Catholic forces who wanted to remove Northern Ireland from British control and unite the island in a single country wanted a distinctively Irish anthem. They chose to put to music a poem by Davis, "A Nation Once Again," that had appeared in the *Nation* and that has since become Ireland's unofficial national anthem. It can be found in *A Short History of Ireland* by John O'Beirne Ranelagh.

When boyhood's fire was in my blood,
I read of ancient freemen,
For Greece and Rome who bravely stood,
Three hundred men and threemen.
And then I prayed I yet might see
Our fetters rent in twain,
And Ireland, long a province, be
A nation once again.

A British soldier stands amidst the destruction in riot-torn Belfast in 1969.

moderate Catholic party. The committee took office early in 1974 but collapsed under the pressure of a general strike called by the Protestant Ulster Workers Council.

Two years later, in response to the deaths of two children in Belfast, the Peace People movement was established, most of the leaders being women tired of the constant violence. Although massive marches were held, the stalemate continued—Catholics insisting on a voice in government and Protestants denying it.

In the 1980s the British government, which had maintained that the Republic of Ireland would play no part in the affairs of Northern Ireland, changed its stance. Prime Minister Margaret Thatcher and Irish *taoiseach* (prime minister) Garret FitzGerald agreed that both countries should cooperate in seeking a peaceful solution. Paisley and the Unionists were alarmed but were assured that "any change in the status of Northern Ireland would only come about with the consent of a majority of the people in Northern Ireland,"[15] a position that became a cornerstone for peace talks.

Another important step was taken in 1992 when Peter Brooke, Britain's chief official in Northern Ireland, suggested that Sinn Féin, the political wing of the IRA, could be included in negotiations provided the IRA called a cease-fire. After two more years of delicate talks, the cease-fire was announced on August 31, 1994, and Sinn Féin president Gerry Adams held his first official meeting with government officials.

THE HUNGER STRIKE

In 1980 Irish Republican Army members imprisoned in Belfast went on a hunger strike seeking to be granted status as political prisoners rather than common criminals. British prime minister Margaret Thatcher was adamantly opposed, saying,

> Let me make one point about the hunger strike in the Maze Prison. I want this to be utterly clear. There can be no political justification for murder or any other crime. The government will never concede political status to the hunger strikers or to any others convicted of criminal offenses in the Province.

The first hunger strike was called off when the British made some vague promises, but another began in 1981, led by Bobby Sands, brother of Bernadette Devlin. Sands began his strike on March 1 and was joined by nine other prisoners. As they grew weaker, pressure—both from within Ireland and throughout the world—mounted on Thatcher. The pope prayed publicly for a solution. Even Thatcher's strongest ally, U.S. president Ronald Reagan, expressed concern.

Thatcher would not budge. When Sands, who had been elected to the British Parliament while in the middle of his strike, died on May 5, Thatcher said, "Mr. Sands was a convicted criminal. He chose to take his own life. It was a choice that his organisation did not allow to many of its victims."

In the end, all ten hunger strikers died, the last—Michael Devine—on August 30. In the words of author Tim Pat Coogan in his book *The Troubles* (from which Thatcher's quotes are also taken), Thatcher had won the battle of the hunger strikers but had lost the war:

> The victory was to prove a pyrrhic [self-defeating] one not only for her policy but for the cause of unionism. Against the accusations of racketeering, drugs-dealing and godfathering, the IRA could now make the irrefutable point: the Mafia don't starve themselves to death for an ideal.

The road to peace was still full of pitfalls. Neither the IRA nor the Protestant militants would agree to decommissioning, the handing over of all weapons. Paisley and his Democratic Unionist Party refused to consider any concessions to Catholics. Finally, an exasperated Adams pulled out of the talks in June 1995. Six months later the IRA cease-fire ended when a bomb killed two people and injured dozens at a London wharf.

U.S. INVOLVEMENT

In the meantime, however, another player—the United States—had taken a role in the search for a peaceful solution. Senator Ted Kennedy of Massachusetts and his sister, Jean Kennedy Smith, named U.S. ambassador to the Republic of Ireland in 1993, had convinced President Bill Clinton that he could play a major role in world history by contributing to peace in Northern Ireland. Clinton acted decisively, going against the wishes of both the British government and his own State Department by granting a visa for Gerry Adams to attend a conference in New York in 1994. The Sinn Féin leader was also included in a St. Patrick's Day celebration at

Irish Prime Minister Garret FitzGerald and British Prime Minister Margaret Thatcher sign the Anglo-Irish agreement in 1985. The agreement pledged both countries to work for peace in Northern Ireland.

THE "HARD" PEOPLE

In 1987 one of the bloodiest episodes of the Troubles occurred when an IRA bomb killed eleven civilians at Enniskillen in County Fermanagh. Gordon Wilson, father of one of the victims, publicly forgave the killers and vowed to work for peace. Later, he met with two IRA spokespersons. This excerpt from the *Irish Times* recounts his meeting and is found in *A Short History of Ireland* by John O'Beirne Ranelagh.

I was there to say, for God's sake, boys, enough is enough. And I got a point blank response. Nothing. . . . They presented me with a typed sheet of paper stating again that they were sorry about Enniskillen and my daughter, and repeated they were not the aggressors, but responded to British aggression. In two words, what they said was, Brits out. And I said, do you mean Protestants? and they said oh no, we would hope to win Protestants over to our way of thinking. I said, but you have driven Protestants away, you haven't won over a single Protestant in 24 years and 3,000 dead. I challenged them why, if their targets were the army and the police, they had killed, in Enniskillen, 11 gentle folk? . . . And they said, that was a mistake. I said, I am tired of hearing the IRA talking about their mistakes. . . . People had told me they couldn't think of anybody more likely to get something from the IRA in the way of a little peace. I thought I might, if only a change of emphasis. I was wrong.

the White House in 1995, along with representatives of other Irish parties, including Unionists. On that occasion, Clinton vowed to "be a friend to Ireland, not merely on St. Patrick's Day, but every day of the year." [16]

Clinton had already made a major contribution by appointing former U.S. senator George Mitchell as a special economic envoy to Ireland in 1994. Mitchell impressed all sides—Irish, British, Catholic, and Protestant—with his patience and skill in bringing persons of opposing viewpoints into agreement. Thus, it was no surprise that in 1995 he was named chairman of an international commission to bring an end to violence in Northern Ireland.

Mitchell's plan called for an election in Northern Ireland on May 30, 1996. The ten political parties receiving the most

Gerry Adams (seen here with Ted Kennedy on the right) is the president of Sinn Féin.

votes would be invited to participate in talks, but only if they demonstrated an opposition to violence. Sinn Féin took 15 percent of the vote—its best showing ever—but was barred from the negotiations because of having ended its cease-fire.

THE SECOND CEASE-FIRE

The talks got back on track in 1997 after Tony Blair, whose Labour Party was much more open to mending fences with Sinn Féin than the Conservatives, became prime minister of Great Britain. Contacts were resumed with Gerry Adams, and the IRA declared a second cease-fire on July 20. On September 9, Sinn Féin accepted the principle that only peaceful means would be used to find a political solution, and the chances for a settlement looked brighter than ever before.

There was still a long way to go. The talks threatened to break down when a Unionist paramilitary leader was murdered in prison and a number of Catholics were killed across Ireland in reprisal. The crisis was averted when Margaret "Mo" Mowland, British secretary of state for Northern Ireland, courageously went into the infamous Maze Prison in Belfast and personally convinced the leaders of the Protestant Ulster Defense Association and Ulster Freedom Fighters to back the peace process, even though Rev. Paisley had withdrawn his Democratic Unionist Party from the talks when Sinn Féin was included.

More trouble lay ahead. First the Protestant Ulster Democratic Party and then Sinn Féin were expelled from the talks following violence by their paramilitary wings, but both returned after peace was restored. Still, the negotiations appeared to be stuck on such points as decommissioning of weapons and the degree of Catholic representation in a new government.

Finally, on March 26, 1998, Mitchell attempted to jumpstart the talks. He set April 9 as a deadline for finding an agreement. When that day came, there was still no accord, but negotiations went on around the clock. Both Blair and Republic *taoiseach* Bertie Ahern came to Belfast to help. "I felt the hand of history on our shoulders," Blair said. "Maybe even with the best will in the world we can't do it, but it's right to try." [17] At last, on Friday, April 10, an agreement was reached and signed. The lives of 3,249 people had been lost over three decades of violence. At least ten times that number had been wounded.

Under the agreement, a new Assembly would be elected from all parties—with Catholics guaranteed representation—to govern Northern Ireland. A North-South Council, representing both Northern Ireland and the Republic, would be formed to deal with common issues such as transportation and agriculture. A bill of rights would be drawn up to protect minority rights, and the RUC would be reformed to include

Irish Prime Minister Bertie Ahern (left) and British Prime Minister Tony Blair helped to forge the Good Friday agreement in 1998. Both continue to pledge support to the peace process.

more Catholics. Sentences of imprisoned terrorists on both sides would be examined and releases made possible. A plan would also be drawn up within two years for decommissioning of weapons on both sides.

DUBLIN'S CONCESSIONS

All parties reaffirmed the position that the political fate of Northern Ireland would be decided only by a majority of its people. The major concession by the Dublin government was that the Republic would drop the two articles in its 1937 constitution asserting that it was the Republic's right to rule the entire island and its duty to seek unification.

The agreement still had to be approved by the voters of Northern Ireland and the Republic in separate referenda on May 22. It was a strange campaign in many ways, not the least of which was to see Gerry Adams and Ulster Unionist Party president David Trimble on the same side of an issue. Although they had both participated in the talks, Trimble had refused any face-to-face meeting with the Sinn Féin leader.

David Trimble (left), president of the Ulster Unionist Party, supported the Good Friday agreement even though the Reverend Ian Paisley (right) vowed to overturn it.

Despite condemnation of the agreement by Paisley, the people overwhelmingly approved it: 71 percent in Northern Ireland and more than 90 percent in the Republic. "People have been worn down by violence," said Londonderry mayor Martin Bradley. "They now realize there is no need for it, and see the economic benefit for living together." [18]

The next hurdle was the Assembly election on June 25. Rev. Paisley, perhaps sensing he had made a mistake in pulling his party out of the talks that led to the Good Friday agreement, vowed to win enough seats to overturn the entire peace process, which he said "has to be brought to a standstill." [19] His party, however, wound up with 19 of the 108 Assembly seats, enough to be disruptive but not enough for control. Trimble's Ulster Unionist Party won 29 seats, the SDLP 25, Sinn Féin 17, and five minor parties won a total of 18.

The people had spoken, but everyone knew there were some who would not listen, those for whom violence had become an end unto itself. "It's like the old dog," one man told a reporter. "If you've been kicked into the corner for 50 years, you learn to be skeptical. There's a long road ahead and plenty of wee fellas up in lofts planning their next moves." [20] Yet, there was also a feeling that this was the best chance ever for an end to the Troubles, and that if peace did not come now, it might not come for generations. Gerry McConville, a former IRA member once imprisoned by the British, talks about a peace settlement in terms of his ten-year-old daughter: "If this conflict does not come to an end, I will be visiting her either in prison or the graveyard. It has to end." [21]

5

Seeing the Ages of Ireland

The past is never far away in Ireland. In Galway City, a modern shopping center has incorporated part of the ancient city walls. In Dublin Castle, government computer terminals glow through windows of a tower built in 1234. In Waterford, buildings of glass and steel rise alongside Reginald's Tower, built by the Vikings using the first mortar in Ireland—a mixture of sand, horsehair, and blood.

The past is important to the Irish, and they have taken great care to preserve and, in some cases, to re-create it. As a result, visitors can follow the footsteps of history along a trail of more than five thousand years.

The Stone Age—Newgrange

In 1699 Charles Campbell, a farmer in County Meath, decided to build a road across his field. Cutting into the side of a low hill, workmen discovered a passage lined with stones, some of which bore strange carvings. Work stopped, and scholars were invited to examine Campbell's find. They were unimpressed, dismissing it as merely a crude pagan tomb, probably of Viking origin.

Not until two hundred years later was it determined that the tomb, Newgrange, not only predates the Vikings but is even older than the great pyramids of Egypt. Built in about 3200 B.C., it is the largest and best-preserved Stone Age passage grave in Europe. Thanks to painstaking excavation and restoration by Professor M. J. O'Kelly from 1962 to 1975, Newgrange stands today, high on a hill above the River Boyne, almost exactly as it appeared five thousand years ago. Nearly all the stones—the ninety-seven giant curbstones, the white quartz sparkling in the sunlight—are original.

The huge mound covers three small burial chambers at the end of a passageway sixty-two feet long but so narrow that visitors must turn their shoulders to squeeze through. No one knows whose bones were placed in the chambers, but they must have been persons of great importance. The early Celts thought Newgrange had been built by the gods and consequently left it alone.

Likewise, no one has been able to agree on an interpretation of the carvings, particularly the interlocking spiral designs. Most experts think they may have something to do with sun worship. This theory makes sense when taken into account with what happens at Newgrange every December 21—the winter solstice, or shortest day of the year.

On that morning, and on the two mornings before and after, the rising sun sends a shaft of light creeping down the passageway to illuminate the burial chamber. As the sun rises, the light recedes, the entire process lasting seventeen minutes. Perhaps the builders wanted to connect those buried in Newgrange with the gradual lengthening of the days and the rebirth of spring.

Today visitors can experience this phenomenon second-hand when guides extinguish lights in the burial chamber and turn on a light that shines up the passageway. Only a very fortunate few can arrange to actually be in the chamber at the winter solstice. As of the fall of 1998, reservations had been made through 2006, and if the day on which one has made arrangements happens to be cloudy—too bad.

BRONZE AND IRON AGES—CRAGGAUNOWEN

The large aspects of ancient civilizations are sometimes all that remain intact—great monuments, castles, and churches—seldom the humble dwellings of everyday people. Early Celtic Ireland is no exception. But while the original wooden structures have long vanished, they have been faithfully re-created in County Clare at Craggaunowen, where visitors can see where and how people lived.

The Craggaunowen Project was the brainchild of the late art historian and archaeologist John Hunt. While helping to restore and furnish Bunratty Castle, he had the idea of bringing the more ancient past to life by building the type of houses that would have existed two thousand years ago, complete with costumed guides who demonstrate what life was like.

The dominant features of the early Celtic landscape were the crannog and the ring fort, and reconstructions of both

DUN AENGUS

For centuries the Aran Islands—Inishmore, Inishmaan, and Inisheer—were the end of the civilized world. Far out in Galway Bay off the western coast of Ireland, they were the most remote place in Europe and one of the most desolate.

The islands' very desolation, however, made them attractive to people trying to escape. Celtic tribes, forced from their own lands by other tribes, found refuge there. Later, Christian monks found a refuge from the world—a place where they could meditate and study.

The largest of the Aran Islands, Inishmore, is only eight miles long and two miles wide, but it contains a wealth of ancient buildings, including Dun Aengus, one of the most spectacular sites in all Ireland.

Dun Aengus is not easy to reach. Most visitors take a ferry from Galway or Rossaveal to Kilronan, the island's only village, and then either a tour van or a pony cart to a pub and souvenir shop at the foot of a hill. From there it is only about a mile and a half to Dun Aengus, but it is all uphill and over tricky limestone outcroppings.

Whoever built Dun Aengus did not want it to be easy to reach or, once there, easy to enter. The Bronze Age fort is perched on the edge of a sheer, three-hundred-foot cliff against which the Atlantic Ocean pounds. There are four concentric stone walls surrounded by a cheval-de-frise, rows of sharp-pointed stone stakes.

Dun Aengus is one of Ireland's great mysteries. No one knows who built it, when it was built, or why. Standing inside the last stone semicircle, looking out at the ocean, visitors cannot help but wonder what would make people so fearful that they would come so far and build something so strong.

can be seen at Craggaunowen. The crannog consists of a wooden palisade built on an artificial island. The islands were built by dragging huge logs to the middle of shallow lakes, driving them into the bottom in a circle, then filling the circle with earth and small stones until an island was formed. The island at Craggaunowen is only about fifty feet from the shore and is connected by a bridge. Two thousand years ago, however, a crannog would have been fifty to one hundred yards from the shore, and there would have been no bridge. Access would have been either by boat or by a series of stepping stones, the surfaces of which were just below the water to make them invisible to any enemy.

When shallow water was unavailable, the early Celts built ring forts, which were much like crannogs except that the wooden walls were built atop banks made of earth or stones. Dwellings inside would most likely be built of interlaced branches packed with clay or mud and roofs of reed or straw thatch. The roofs, kept free of insects by smoke from fires inside the houses, would have lasted fifty years or more.

Another outstanding feature at Craggaunowen is a *fulachta fiadh*, the Celtic version of the backyard barbecue. It consists of a wood-lined pit into which groundwater has seeped. Stones would be heated red-hot and dumped into the pit until the water boiled, at which point meat wrapped in straw was put into the pit to cook.

Professor O'Kelly of Newgrange fame once put a similar *fulachta fiadh* in County Cork to the test. He was successful in cooking a ten-pound leg of mutton, but concluded that the ancient Celts must have had great patience. It took him an hour and a half to boil the water with hot stones and another three and a half hours to properly cook the meat.

THE MONASTIC MOVEMENT—CLONMACNOISE

It is hard to imagine today, particularly while navigating the narrow, twisting roads to Clonmacnoise, that it was once the crossroads of Ireland. The River Shannon runs north-south and a ridge of gravel left thousands of years ago by a retreating glacier runs east-west across the boglands of County Offaly. It was a natural spot, therefore, for the foundation of a monastery in 548 by St. Ciaran.

Clonmacnoise was a center of learning and theology for more than one thousand years, until it was reduced to a ruin by English soldiers. Even the ruins, however, are most impressive—seven churches, two round towers, and one of the finest crosses in Ireland.

The cross, known as "the Cross of the Scriptures," is covered with carvings depicting biblical scenes and was used by the monks to teach rural people in an era when books were rare. Since the artists had no idea how biblical figures appeared, they had to draw on their own experiences. Roman soldiers, for instance, are pictured wearing the horned helmets of Vikings.

Clonmacnoise was an educational and religious center in Ireland until it was destroyed by the English in the sixteenth century.

Vikings were also the inspiration for the round towers, which survive in many places in Ireland. From their heights, often more than one hundred feet, lookouts could spot the invading hordes and warn the community below. Monks then would take refuge in the tower, carrying gold crucifixes, chalices, and other treasures through a series of trapdoors, pulling ladders up after them. Sometimes, this worked; on other occasions, however, the Vikings discovered that the towers made excellent chimneys.

The smallest of the churches—only nine by twelve feet— is nevertheless the most important because it is the tomb of St. Ciaran. Although the saint died less than a year after establishing Clonmacnoise, his inspiration was so great that those who came after him spread their learning, not only throughout Ireland but also as far away as Poland, converting that country to Christianity. A shelter on the grounds marks the spot where Pope John Paul II, a native of Poland, held a special service in St. Ciaran's honor in 1979.

The saint's grave has long been a destination for pilgrims, and soil from the church floor was thought to have magical powers. So much of the soil was taken that a stone floor eventually was laid. People then began taking handfuls of earth from outside the church, and as recently as 1998 farmers would steal into Clonmacnoise by night, removing bits of turf to be placed in corners of their fields to ward off cattle diseases.

THE CELTIC NATION—CASHEL

The Rock of Cashel is perhaps the most impressive sight in Ireland. The collection of medieval buildings perched atop a two-hundred-foot-high limestone hill dominates the County

THE *BRENDAN*

Most people think Christopher Columbus discovered America in 1492; others claim Viking sailors reached North America in about the year 1000. The Irish, however, will tell you that St. Brendan, a historical figure born in about 490 A.D., sailed to the New World in a boat made of ox hides stretched over a wooden frame.

According to the story, St. Brendan and his crew spent seven years on the voyage, encountering an island of sheep (perhaps the Hebrides), an island of thunderbolts (possibly volcanic Iceland), and a crystal column (perhaps an iceberg). The story was a favorite in the Middle Ages not only in Ireland but also throughout Europe. To see if it might be true, explorer Tim Severin decided to build a boat based on descriptions in the legend.

Severin and his crew set sail on May 17, 1976. Thirteen months later they reached the coast of Newfoundland, proving it might have been possible for St. Brendan to have done so sometime in the 500s. It was a rugged voyage. Several times the hull of the boat was pierced by floating ice. Crew members had to hang over the side, sprayed by freezing water, and sew on patches of leather.

Severin named his boat the *Brendan* after the saint. It is now on display at Craggaunowen. The voyage of the *Brendan* provided the material for a cover story in *National Geographic* magazine (December 1977).

Tipperary countryside much the same way it has for more than fifteen hundred years.

Cashel—from the Irish word *caisel,* or fortress—was the stronghold of the Eoghanacht kings of Munster and later the Dál Cais kings, including Brian Boru, who called himself king of Cashel. In 1101 the site was given to the church, and it remained the headquarters of the bishop of Cashel until 1752.

Cashel's association with Christianity, however, goes back much further. In about 435 St. Patrick supposedly came to Cashel and converted the king of Munster. The story goes that at one point during the baptism ceremony, St. Patrick accidentally drove the sharp end of his staff through the monarch's foot. The king, thinking it was part of the ceremony, never flinched.

The Rock of Cashel, a collection of ancient buildings that sits on a 200-foot cliff, was once a stronghold of the kings of Munster.

The most celebrated building at the Rock of Cashel is Cormac's Chapel, the earliest and finest Romanesque church in Ireland. Unlike the surrounding structures, it was built entirely of stone—even the roof—and thus could not be burned by Oliver Cromwell's troops in the 1600s.

Cashel had scores of bishops in its long history, but none was as notorious as Miler Magrath, although plenty were probably more holy. In 1571 England's Queen Elizabeth I appointed Magrath the Protestant archbishop of Cashel. He continued, however, to act as the Roman Catholic bishop of Down, in Ulster, and apparently was able to keep this dual existence secret.

When he died in 1621 at the age of one hundred, he was buried in the walls of the cathedral at Cashel. His self-composed epitaph, still clearly visible, reads:

> The Ode of Miler Magrath, Archbishop of Cashel, to
> the passer by:
> Patrick, the Glory of our Isle and Gown,
> First sat a Bishop in the See of Down,
> I wish that I succeeding him in place
> As Bishop, had an equal share of Grace,
> I serv'd thee, England, fifty years in Jars
> And pleased thy Princes in the midst of Wars;
> Here where I'm placed I'm not; and thus the case is,
> I'm not in both, yet am in both the places. [22]

Magrath became a wealthy man from the revenue of both his bishoprics, and both thought they would benefit from his will. Neither one did. He left his entire fortune to his two wives and nine children.

THE NORMAN TRIUMPH—KING JOHN'S CASTLE

Unlike the Vikings before them, the Normans who began their conquest of Ireland in 1169 did not cluster in coastal towns and seek to control trade; they set out to cover the entire island. Dozens of grim, gray castles bear witness to how they hoped to survive in and dominate a hostile countryside. King John's Castle in Limerick City is an outstanding example.

For almost eight hundred years the castle has dominated Limerick from its position on a small island formed by a loop of the River Shannon. Viking settlers recognized the spot as a natural defensive position and erected some earthworks to enclose their wooden houses. The Normans employed those same fortifications in building the castle, which takes its name not because King John of England lived there but because he granted the city a royal charter and in 1200 ordered the castle built.

THE BOOK OF KELLS

The most prized possession of any medieval church or monastery was its Bible. No expense was too great nor time period too long in which to make Bibles as beautiful as possible. A common practice was to make the first word or words of each book of the Bible as elaborate as possible—richly decorated with color and gold leaf in a process known as illumination. The Book of Kells, on display at the Old Library at Trinity College in Dublin, is the most outstanding example of an early illuminated manuscript in Ireland and one of the finest in the world.

Full of intricate designs, mythical animals, and mysterious symbols, the Book of Kells—actually four bound volumes—contains the four gospels. It was not produced at Kells, a monastic settlement in County Meath, but probably on Iona, an island off the coast of Scotland. Some experts think it was produced in about the year 800 to mark the two hundredth anniversary of the death of St. Columba, the Irish monk who founded Iona. In 836 a Viking raid forced the monks of Iona to flee to Kells in Ireland, taking the precious manuscript with them.

In 1006 or 1007, according to the Annals of Ulster, as quoted in *Exploring the Book of Kells* by George Otto Sims, the book, described as "the chief treasure of the western world . . . was stolen by night from the western sacristy of the great stone church of Cenannus [Kells]." The thieves did not want the book itself, but instead the golden case in which it had been placed. The book was recovered two months later.

The monastery at Kells was closed in the 1100s, and the book was the property of the parish church there until it was moved to Trinity College in 1661. Since the mid-1800s it has been displayed to the public in the Old Library. It is kept in an air-tight case, and only two pages at a time—an illustrated page and a page of text—are on view.

An illustration from the Book of Kells.

Approaching the castle from across the Shannon, it is easy to see how it would have inspired both fear and respect. The high walls, up to fifteen feet thick, and the rounded corner towers were built to withstand the latest siege tactics. In the unlikely event invaders forced their way over the moat and drawbridge, for instance, the only entrance was a portcullis, or iron gate, housed in a tunnel flanked by two towers. Anyone trying to force their way through the gate would be showered with arrows, stones, and boiling tar from the towers and through holes in the ceiling of the tunnel.

The battlements offer a spectacular view of the Shannon and the main part of the city on the opposite bank, and it was partially to guard against attack from the city that the castle was built. The strongest fortifications are on the west side, facing what came to be known as Irish Town. The area behind the castle to the east was walled in and called English Town. Perhaps nowhere in Ireland is there a more striking example of the division between the conquerors and the conquered.

Visitors to King John's Castle need not imagine what the interior would have been like in the 1200s. It has been faithfully re-created, complete with the tents of costumed artisans and

Structures like King John's Castle are ancient reminders of the Anglo-Norman conquest.

laborers eager to describe their work. Even King John himself awaits in the northeast tower in the form of a costumed mannequin who carries on a conversation with an unseen interrogator. In a petulant voice, the man commonly considered the worst king in English history attempts to defend himself, but he's not very convincing.

King John's Castle was an impregnable fortress long after the end of the Norman era. Between 1691 and 1692 it was the last refuge for the troops of the deposed King James II of England. It withstood two sieges, and only the abandonment of Ireland by James and his French allies induced the defenders to surrender.

THE PROTESTANT ASCENDANCY—FLORENCE COURT

The surrender of King John's Castle and the subsequent Treaty of Limerick ended more than 150 years of religious wars and put control of Ireland firmly in the hands of an elite Protestant minority. The 1700s were years of Protestant prosperity, the outward signs of which were the magnificent Georgian (so-called for a series of four Georges who ruled England) manor houses such as Florence Court.

No family in Ireland had a stronger Protestant pedigree than the Coles of County Fermanagh. William Cole, a country squire from Devonshire, England, raised a troop of cavalry for service in Elizabeth I's Irish wars in the late 1500s. He was a leading figure in the plantation of Protestants in Ulster and was rewarded by Elizabeth's successor, James I, with extensive lands that he ruled from Enniskillen Castle.

The family's fortunes continued to rise. William's great-grandson, John, was knighted for his service to King William III. His great-great-grandson was made a baron, and his great-great-great-grandson was granted the title first earl of Enniskillen. By this time, however, living in an ancient castle was no longer comfortable or fashionable. A fire at Enniskillen Castle prompted John Cole to begin building a country house, which he named for his wife, Florence.

Work began on the house in 1716 and continued under three generations of Coles until it was finally completed in the late 1770s. The result is a three-story central block, its exterior "a happy, if unscholarly collection of rusticated corners and window-surrounds, pediments, brackets, and keystones," [23] flanked by two colonnaded wings.

BLARNEY

Of all the castles in Ireland, Blarney Castle is the best known and most visited. It is not of any great historical or architectural significance, yet every year tens of thousands of tourists line up to climb to the top of the battlements, grasp a rail, lean backwards over the top of the parapet, and kiss the underside of a rock—the famous Blarney stone.

The first stone castle was built on the site in 1210, and the present structure was completed by Dermot McCarthy, king of Munster, in 1446. The stone was given to Dermot's ancestor, Cormac Tiege McCarthy, by the Scottish king Robert the Bruce in 1314 for his help in defeating the English at the battle of Bannockburn. It is supposedly half of the Stone of Scone, on which the kings of Scotland were seated to be crowned.

In the 1500s Queen Elizabeth I of England sought promises from the Irish chiefs that they would hold their lands under title from her. Cormac McCarthy, then lord of Blarney, sent her letter after letter, all very polite and eloquent, yet never quite agreeing to comply with her wishes. The story goes that finally the exasperated queen flung his latest letter to the floor and exclaimed that it was "a lot of Blarney talk."

The word thus passed into the English language, meaning skillful, empty flattery. Kissing the stone, legend has it, will give one the gift of eloquence.

Blarney Castle is home to the world famous Blarney Stone.

The real glory of Florence Court, however, is the interior, particularly the elaborate display of plasterwork on the walls and ceilings, generally regarded as the finest in Ireland. The intricate decorations, which include flowers, masks, animals, and figures from mythology, give the interior a lightness missing from the exterior view.

Everything about Florence Court fairly shouts power, wealth, and Protestantism. Portraits of ancestors line walls and staircases. Decorations include cannonballs from the siege of Derry, a Protestant victory still celebrated in Northern Ireland; a musket presented to the third earl as grand master of the Protestant Orange Order; and ornate trunks that once belonged to William III and Queen Mary.

At its zenith Florence Court was surrounded by gardens and grounds covering 30,000 acres. Eighty servants were required—twenty-five in the kitchen, twenty-five upstairs, and thirty gardeners. As the Penal Laws against Catholics were relaxed, it became profitable for the Coles to sell pieces of their holdings to tenant farmers. Consequently, only 280 acres of the estate remain, and they and the house were donated to the government in 1954, although the family continued to live there until 1989. The present earl, ten generations removed from William Cole, chose not to live in Florence Court, but the influence of his ancestors continues to echo through its hallways.

LAYERS OF HISTORY

Remnants of Ireland's past exist, side by side, with one another and with modern structures. The past is also frequently piled on top of itself and is a constant source of surprises as it unfolds, layer by layer. Every excavation and every construction project seems to turn up—literally—new discoveries.

No building in Ireland, for instance, has been more thoroughly studied, explored, added onto, and renovated than Dublin Castle—the center of Irish government since the 1230s. It was here that King Richard II of England accepted the surrender of the Irish kings in 1394. It was here that the attack of Silken Thomas, earl of Kildare, failed in 1534, opening the way for an English occupation of Dublin that lasted until 1922. It was here that King James II spent the night after his disastrous defeat at the Boyne in 1690. It was here that the wounded James Connolly was taken during the Easter Rising of 1916 and was both treated and sentenced to death.

TARA

Most people connect the name Tara with Scarlett O'Hara's plantation in Margaret Mitchell's novel *Gone with the Wind*. The real Tara, however, is one of the most important and storied places in Irish history—both ancient and modern.

The Hill of Tara, high above the River Boyne valley, was chosen by Stone Age people for a passage grave. Later, Iron Age people built ring forts atop the hill. One, named the Royal Enclosure, contains a standing stone about three feet high. It was at this Lialh Fail, or Stone of Destiny, that the high kings of Ireland were crowned until the 1000s.

The symbolism of Tara was employed by Daniel O'Connell in 1843 when he chose it as the site for one of his "monster meetings," mass demonstrations designed to force Great Britain to dissolve the Act of Union that had made Ireland part of the United Kingdom in 1801. On August 15 a crowd reported to be more than 1 million people covered the grassy hill to hear O'Connell speak. This excerpt from a contemporary observer is found in *The Course of Irish History*, edited by T. W. Moody and F. X. Martin.

> Before the procession had arrived within a dozen miles of the historic hill large crowds were discovered who had come from distant places during the night, and bivouacked [camped] in the green pastures of Meath, under a genial August sky. . . . Three miles from the hill the vehicles had to be abandoned; from the immensity of the attendance there was space only for footmen. . . . The procession however was but a river discharging itself into an ocean. The whole district was covered with men. The population within a day's march began to arrive on foot shortly before daybreak, and continued to arrive, on all sides, and by every available approach, till noon. It was impossible from any one point to see the entire meeting. . . . Hill and plain were covered with a multitude countless as the bearded grain. . . . It was ordinarily spoken of as a million, and was certainly a muster of men such as had never before assembled in one place in Ireland, in peace or war.

Yet, even as the twentieth century approached, Dublin Castle had not yielded all its secrets. In 1986 the River Poddle, along whose banks the castle once stood but which is

Dublin Castle, the center of Irish government for centuries, is one of the most studied buildings in Ireland.

now completely underground, rose and flooded the lower rooms of the Gunpowder Tower. When the water was pumped out, workers examining the foundations made a startling discovery—a remnant of the wall of the original Viking fort that had been built on the site in about 842. Another of the many layers of Irish history had revealed itself.

A People
in Transition

The term *developing nation* normally calls forth images of countries in Latin America, Africa, or Asia that are mostly rural, have widespread poverty, lack industry, and are emerging from centuries of colonialism. While Ireland certainly cannot be classified as backward or impoverished, it nevertheless is developing as a player on the global scene. Only since the 1950s have the Irish, both north and south, begun to come out from under the shadow of British rule. They are slowly freeing themselves of the bonds of the past and finding their identity as a people.

The challenge for the Irish is not to break their ties with Britain. That would be impossible and impractical given the extent and length of British influence and its proximity. Rather, the challenge is to blend the best aspects of their own culture with the best of the British legacy.

As the twentieth century loomed ahead, the Irish seemed to be meeting this challenge. In areas of life from business to religion, institutions emerged that were uniquely Irish in character—not the Ireland of a hundred years ago, but a new, vital, modern Ireland.

Above everything hangs the question of unification. If Ireland can avoid the self-destructive tendencies of the past, it may finally be ready to put aside centuries of division and of an inferior national image to become an equal partner in world affairs with its larger neighbor and with the rest of Europe.

GOVERNMENT

The government of the Republic is, like Great Britain, a parliamentary democracy. The legislative body, the Oireachteas, consists of two houses. The 166 members of the Dáil are elected by direct popular vote, while the 60 members of the

Seanad (Senate) are either appointed by the *taoiseach* (prime minister) or elected by special interest groups, including universities.

The *taoiseach* is the leader of the political party that either holds a majority of seats in the Dáil or is the larger of a combination of parties that agree to govern in a coalition. Two of the major parties have their roots in the conflict over the ratification of the 1922 treaty with Great Britain. The protreaty faction of Arthur Griffith and Michael Collins became Fine Gael (Tribes of Gael), while the antitreaty followers of Eamon De Valera became Fianna Fáil. The third major party, Labour, has frequently taken part in coalition governments but has never had a clear majority on its own. The bulk of political power rests in the Dáil. The Seanad may delay legislation for up to ninety days but cannot block or veto bills passed by the Dáil.

Elections to the Dáil are conducted at least every five years but may be called in the interim if the party in power feels it no longer has a working majority or if it thinks it can increase its majority. In such cases the president, on instructions from the *taoiseach*, dissolves the Oireachtas and calls nationwide elections.

The post of president of the Republic is largely ceremonial. Presidents are elected every seven years and may serve two consecutive terms. Although they have no direct voice in government, Irish presidents can be very influential. Both Mary Robinson, elected Ireland's first woman president in

(From left) Mary McAleese, Prime Minister Bertie Ahern, Deputy Prime Minister Mary Harney, and Martin McAleese. Mary McAleese is the second woman in Irish history to be elected president.

1990, and her successor, Mary McAleese, have helped shape public opinion, especially on family and moral issues.

The Republic's government is highly centralized. Ninety percent of public spending is by the national government, and there is no local control over some functions, including education and police. As a result, the Dáil tends to get bogged down in local administrative issues critical to the voters in their home districts while giving little attention to national policies.

What local government exists is in the hands of thirty-eight city corporations or county councils. These councils are elected by popular vote and administer such functions as housing, libraries, water and sewage, and health services. No local government exists for towns or villages, however. As a result many Irish feel alienated from their government since all decisions are made either sixty miles away in the county capital or a hundred miles away in Dublin.

The government of Northern Ireland is completely different. As a part of Great Britain, it sends representatives to Parliament in London and, until 1972 and the era of direct rule from Britain, to a separate parliament in Belfast that had jurisdiction over purely local issues. Under the Good Friday agreement of 1998, however, local government in Northern Ireland is vested in a 108-member Assembly, elected for the first time on June 25.

Historically, the Ulster Unionist Party dominated politics in Northern Ireland, with election laws and districts arranged to keep the Protestant, pro-British party in power. The Good Friday agreement overturned the system and introduced proportional voting whereby a party earning 40 percent of the vote would be guaranteed 40 percent of the seats in the Assembly. This not only guaranteed representation from the Catholic Social Democrat and Labor Party, Sinn Féin, and the right-wing Protestant Democratic Unionist Party of Rev. Ian Paisley, but it also allowed representation from a host of smaller parties. Consequently, nine parties made up the first Assembly.

RELIGION

Religion plays a more prominent role in Ireland than in any other country of western Europe. Although no longer completely dominant, the Roman Catholic Church remains a

Pope John Paul II remains a figure of great reverence in Ireland, considered the most traditionally Catholic country in the world.

powerful influence over how the people of the Republic live. And, sadly, the conflict between Catholics and Protestants in Northern Ireland continues to mean that many people die violently.

The Republic of Ireland is the most strongly Roman Catholic country in the world, and Pope John Paul II is said to consider it the last area of traditional Catholicism in Europe. More than 95 percent of the population are baptized Catholics. Regular attendance at mass, once more than 90 percent, has fallen to 82 percent, but that is still remarkable when compared with 14 percent in supposedly Catholic France. Faith is especially strong in the rural west, where crucifixes and pictures of the pope are sold in stores alongside postcards, and where shrines can be found on the sides of country lanes.

Two main reasons why Catholicism is so strong in Ireland have been suggested by historians and theologians. First, its mysticism and ceremony seem to have great appeal to the Celtic character with its legacy of magic and myths. Second, the determination of the British to deny the Irish their Catholic

The Church and Censorship

The power exerted by the Roman Catholic Church in Irish society can be seen in the degree of censorship of books. Although such censorship is not as widespread as in past decades, the laws permitting it are still in force, and a handful of foreign writers cannot be published in the Republic.

In 1926, soon after the country became independent, the government, pressured by the church, set up a Committee of Enquiry on Evil Literature. The result was the passage of the Censorship of Publications Act of 1929. The intent of the act was to ban pornography, but the influence of the church led to the prohibition of virtually anything dealing with subjects such as homosexuality or birth control. More than twelve hundred books were banned during the 1930s, including works by such authors as George Orwell, Aldous Huxley, and Bertrand Russell.

The censorship act deals only with printed material, but the church has influenced the closing of some plays in the past, including Tennessee Williams's *The Rose Tattoo* in 1955. The producer, Alan Simpson, was arrested and charged with presenting an obscene performance, but the charges were later dropped.

Far fewer books are banned today. The Censorship Board has concentrated on visual printed matter. *Playboy* magazine, for instance, cannot be imported or sold in the Republic.

The church has also employed other forms of censorship. Although James Joyce's *Ulysses* was never officially banned, most booksellers declined to stock it. The Catholic clergy at Clongowes College, negatively portrayed by Joyce in *Portrait of the Artist as a Young Man*, refused to allow his name to be spoken as late as the 1960s. And in 1990 John McGahern's prize-winning novel *Amongst Women* was considered unsuitable by the church, and he was fired from his teaching position at a Catholic school.

faith made it all the stronger. Although the church took almost no active part in the various rebellions, Catholicism became a symbol of resistance.

For centuries Irish Catholics looked to their priests as authoritarian figures instead of to their government. It was natural, therefore, that the church maintained this role after independence. The Irish constitution of 1937 recognized the "special position" of the Catholic Church. Books and plays were heavily censored. Practices that ran counter to church teachings, such as contraception, not only were illegal but could not even be discussed in print. Likewise, politicians routinely consulted leading bishops before proposing legislation.

Much has changed. The recognition of the church in the constitution was removed in 1972, and censorship is largely a thing of the past. Alarmed by the spread of AIDS, the government legalized contraception in 1993 despite the strong objections of the church. After defeating a referendum to legalize divorce in 1986, the Republic approved a similar measure in 1995, but only by a margin of less than half a percent. A referendum to permit abortion, however, was soundly defeated.

Many in Ireland feel the Catholic Church is out of touch with modern society. A frequent criticism is that the rigidly conservative church leaders concentrate almost exclusively on sexual issues and ignore social problems. Also, fewer men are going into the priesthood. In September 1998 St. Peter's Seminary in Wexford closed after 179 years. Enrollment, once more than a hundred, had dwindled to eight.

Although Catholic leaders no longer claim, as one bishop did in 1951, that "God is the author of organized civil society and hence political and social activities are subject to God's moral law, of which the Church is the divinely constituted interpreter and guardian," [24] they have remained firm on moral issues. As Bishop Jeremiah Newman of Limerick notes, "Of course the Church must be authoritarian. Christ gave the Church immutable moral laws, which do not change with mere changes in society." [25]

Protestants, only 3 percent of the population in the south, make up 60 percent in Northern Ireland. The Presbyterians are the leading denomination with about 25 percent, while the Anglican Church of Ireland claims 20 percent and the Methodists and other smaller groups have the remaining 15 percent.

Settlement patterns going back to the plantations of the 1700s and the recent decades of violence have brought about a religiously segregated society. Little social interaction exists between Catholics and Protestants, and couples in mixed marriages are likely to be shunned by both families. In recent years, however, many interfaith and nonsectarian schools have been started by moderates who hope that, by bringing Catholic and Protestant children together, long-standing prejudices can be overcome. Teresa McKeever, a Catholic mother from Londonderry, says, "I can't lose my fears and suspicions overnight. Maybe I never can, but how can my son grow up to hate someone he had such a good time playing with?" [26]

THE ECONOMY

Ireland has always been a poor country. For much of its history it was little more than a British colony, and its economy, rooted in agriculture, provided wealth to an elite group of landlords. The Industrial Revolution, which did so much to make Britain a dominant world power, stopped at the Irish Sea. After independence, Ireland's economy remained stagnant, oddly enough by design; it was only in the last half of the twentieth century—especially after joining the European Union in 1973—that Ireland has moved toward becoming a modern industrialized nation. Still, the Republic's per capita income is only $9,950, the lowest in western Europe and half that of the United States.

Ireland was relatively untouched by the Industrial Revolution and remains a predominantly agricultural country.

Agriculture still is important but occupies a far smaller place in the economy than it did even a few years ago. Less than 14 percent of the workforce in the Republic is in agriculture, compared with 30 percent in the 1960s and 52 percent in 1926. The figure in Northern Ireland is less than 10 percent. Mechanization and a migration of people to the cities have combined to eliminate many small family farms. The number of farms has been more than cut in half—from 264,000 to 120,000 since independence.

Ireland's climate and soil are perfect for growing trees, and forestry is increasing in importance. Once almost covered with forests, Ireland was stripped of its woods over the centuries to make room for pastures and fields. In 1900 barely 1

THE MODERN FARMER

Ireland remains basically a rural country, and farming is still an important part of the economy. Modernization, however, has brought major changes to the countryside. Farms are larger, more mechanized, and employ fewer people. At the same time, the strong sense of community has diminished.

Séan Clarke in County Mayo described how life on his dairy farm had changed in just one generation. His comments are found in *Ireland and the Irish* by John Ardagh.

In the 1950s my parents on this farm had just horses, no car, and no running water—before going to school, I would walk over the fields to draw water from a well for my mother, who made her own butter. We had three cows, and we grew potatoes and vegetables and sold eggs. But this kind of small-scale mixed farming has almost disappeared. It makes no money. We used to scythe the grass for hay—it was back-breaking. Today there is far less of this drudgery, yet I think I work as long hours as my father did, what with all the paperwork. And community life has changed. In the old days, there was so much mutual self-help: as a boy I used to be sent round to other farms to help them pick potatoes or gather grain, and they would do the same for us, all for free. But now people are more separate from each other, more egotistical. You are on your own much more, and you either make it or you don't.

percent of the land was forested. Thanks to a vigorous government program, that figure has increased to 5 percent.

For years after independence, the Republic discouraged heavy industry and investment from outside the country. De Valera especially thought the country should be self-sufficient and "satisfied with frugal comfort." It was only in the 1950s that his successor, Séan Lemass, took action to do away with the protective tariffs that limited imports and to lure foreign investors through tax breaks and grants. Also attractive to investors has been the Irish workforce, which is highly literate and English-speaking. The Republic has since become a major exporter of computer equipment, chemicals, and electronics.

Even so, unemployment continues to be a major problem throughout the Republic, reaching more than 12 percent in 1997. In the south emigration used to offset the traditionally high Catholic birthrate. In the 1980s and 1990s, however, emigration slowed because of poor labor markets in the United

The Titanic *was built in the shipyards of Belfast, Northern Ireland.*

States, Great Britain, and Australia—the favorite destinations of those leaving Ireland. Also contributing to unemployment have been the large number of people migrating from farms to cities and the increasing technological ability of modern industry to lower their number of employees through automation. In addition, some international companies have moved their operations in Ireland to countries such as Indonesia, where labor is far cheaper.

The job market is better in Northern Ireland, but unemployment still is high—around 11.2 percent in 1997. Belfast's giant shipyards—the original *Titanic* was built there—had only a fifth as many workers in 1996 as in 1976. Automation has vastly decreased the number of people making Irish linen, formerly Northern Ireland's largest industry. Foreign companies have been much slower to locate in the north than in the south, mostly because of the constant threat of violence.

The most booming industry in Ireland is tourism. More than 3 million visitors come to the Republic each summer, attracted by the sophisticated marketing techniques of the Bord Fáilte, or national tourism board. The constant media attention given to bombings and shootings in Northern Ireland has largely kept tourists away, and their return would be one of the greatest economic benefits of peace.

EDUCATION

The tradition of teaching and learning is strong in Ireland, going all the way back to early Christian times when Irish monks were the finest and most dedicated teachers in Europe. The hunger for education was strengthened during centuries of British domination when learning was seen as the only method of escape from poverty. As a result the Irish have developed a comprehensive educational system that is taken advantage of by almost all citizens.

Ireland's literacy rate is 98 percent, one of the highest in the world. Children in the south begin school at about age six, and more than 80 percent complete secondary or technical school at age seventeen or eighteen, as compared with 48 percent in England. Primary school lasts six years; then students move on to a secondary school that offers parallel courses in academic and vocational subjects.

At age fifteen all students take junior certificate examinations that determine their next level of courses. At the end of

The Irish Language

The Celtic-based Irish language, Gaelic, was once the everyday tongue of the people of Ireland. Its use gradually declined through centuries of English domination. By 1851 only 25 percent of the people used Irish regularly. By 1912 that number had been reduced to 12 percent. Less than 1 percent of the population claims Irish as a first language, whereas Welsh is the first language of 12 percent of Wales.

Even though the Republic's government actively encourages the teaching and use of Irish—all public signs have to be in both Irish and English, for instance—it recognizes that English is the dominant language. The 1937 constitution states that Irish is the "first official language" of the country while English is the "second official language."

The teaching of Irish in schools has been mandatory since the 1920s, but the emphasis has been somewhat relaxed. Until 1973 no student could graduate from secondary school without at least a passing grade on an Irish exam. Now the exam must be taken but not necessarily passed.

Some universities require at least a slight knowledge of Irish for admission. One that does not is the University of Limerick, whose president, Dr. Edward Walsh, has some strong personal views on the subject, as quoted in John Ardagh's *Ireland and the Irish*.

> I suffered from it in 1972, when for a chair related to nuclear physics I had to sit one paper in Irish; and I failed to get the job just because my Irish was so poor. . . . Ireland used to lose many good scientists in that way—crazy! Fortunately, it happens much less today. . . . But I still think it is wrong to stuff compulsory Irish down pupils' throats. The language is a valuable part of our culture and should be kept alive—but only for those—maybe 10 or 15 percent—who really want to learn and use it and will do so joyously.

secondary school, students take a second set of exams leading to a leaving certificate. These exams cover five to seven subjects, including mathematics, history, science, and languages. Scores on these exams determine which universities students may enter and which major subjects they may study. The study of the Irish language is compulsory, but scores in the examination do not count toward graduation, and many students consider it a waste of time while many in government question its expense.

The educational system in Northern Ireland is based on the British model. A national curriculum has been established, and at age sixteen students take exams in each subject, either O-level exams or the more difficult A-levels. Those passing the exams receive general certificates of secondary education, but those who pass A-levels have two more years of school and yet another set of exams to determine entrance into universities.

As it does in so many areas of Irish life, religion plays a major part in education. Although the majority of the schools are supported by the government, they are run by the churches. Religious education is an integral part of the curriculum. Indeed, official government policy states that "religion should permeate the whole school day."[27] Moderate government officials who have tried to make schools less religious have encountered fierce opposition from both Catholics and Protestants.

Nevertheless, Irish schools are gradually becoming more secular. One reason is the dwindling supply of monks and nuns available to teach. While nuns still make up the bulk of Catholic primary school teachers, only 12 percent of secondary school teachers are in holy orders. Not only are fewer people going into such orders, but many of those who do choose to work do so in slums or in overseas missions rather than teach.

Religious influence is slight at Ireland's universities, both southern and northern. By far the most prestigious is Trinity College in Dublin, which was established by Queen Elizabeth I in 1592. Trinity's graduates include Jonathan Swift, Edmund Burke, Oscar Wilde, Theobald Wolfe Tone, and Samuel Beckett. Other universities in the Republic are University College Dublin, Dublin City University, St. Patrick's College in Maynooth, University College Galway, University College Cork, and the University of Limerick. Only at Maynooth, which includes the largest Catholic seminary in Ireland, is much church influence found.

The two universities of Northern Ireland—Queen's University in Belfast and the University of Ulster—were formerly almost entirely Protestant. Lately, partly to escape the violence, more Protestants have gone to universities in Britain or in the Republic. As a result, enrollment is about evenly split between Catholics and Protestants.

Leisure and Sports

Most of the stereotypes associated with the Irish—brawling, hot-tempered, shiftless, prone to drunkenness—are as false as most stereotypes. One generalization, however, is absolutely accurate—the Irish love a good time and know how to have one. Whether it is in the lively theaters of Dublin, the music-filled pubs, or the sports stadiums rocking with cheers, the Irish display a zest for life and a determination to live it to the fullest.

The center of Irish social life is the public house, or pub. There seems to be a pub everywhere one turns in Ireland— more than twenty thousand in all—and it is a rare village, no

Most Irish gather at the town pub for recreation and socializing.

matter how tiny, that cannot boast at least one. The pub is where people gather not only for entertainment but also to get the news of the day. Television and radio stations are government-owned and national in scope. Newspapers are more local but may cover two or three counties. The pub, therefore, is where one goes to find out the latest gossip.

The pub is also where traditional Irish music is kept alive, especially in the more remote parts of the west. In the pubs of Galway, Mayo, and Donegal, local musicians hold forth with fiddles, harps, tin whistles, pipes, and the *bhrodran*, a goatskin drum drawn over a round frame. The joy of this music is that the players are not necessarily performing for tourists, but for themselves.

Alcoholic beverages are a major factor in Irish society, but they are not as prevalent as some outsiders think. The patrons of pubs seem to be having such a rollicking good time that it perhaps disguises the fact that alcohol consumption is less than in Britain or Germany. Beer is the drink of choice, particularly Guinness, a dark, rich, creamy brew known as stout. To other people, a pint may be a standard unit of measure; to the Irish, it is Guinness.

The exuberance of the Irish extends to sports. Irish sports tend to be fast and violent, not like the staid, slow-paced cricket of the British. Association football (soccer) is highly popular, as is Gaelic football, an Irish version of rugby.

Just as popular as football, however, is hurling, an ancient Irish game in which a ball is carried, hit, or thrown with curved sticks made of ash. Hurling, in fact, is nicknamed "the clash of the ash," but the sticks are just as likely to clash with an arm or leg as a ball. Protective gear is minimal, and injuries are frequent. Legend has it that before the battle of Moytura in ancient Celtic times, a game of hurling was played in which four hundred people were killed.

Hurling is especially popular in the Republic, where each county has a team that—unlike football—is made up of unpaid amateurs. People are passionately attached to their local teams, and on each summer Saturday the roads are filled with cars flying the blue and gold of County Clare or the black and white of County Kildare. Spectator stands are seas of waving flags and a constant roar. Thankfully, the Irish have managed to keep sports in perspective, and spectator vio-

One of the most popular sports in Ireland is Gaelic football.

lence is rare, unlike the hooliganism that can mar sporting events in Britain and the United States.

On a slightly more peaceful note, horse racing is enjoyed throughout the country, as much for a love of the animals as for the excitement of wagering. Also popular is fishing, and some of the best trout streams in the world are to be found in Ireland.

Ireland's literature and music are grounded more in Celtic traditions than in European classicism. Storytelling has occupied an important place since ancient Celtic times, so it is hardly surprising that the theater has been the most vital part of Irish literature or that it has been a primary expression of Irish nationalism.

The centerpiece of Irish drama is Dublin's Abbey Theatre, founded in 1899 as the Irish Literary Theatre by poet and playwright William Butler Yeats and Isabella Augusta, Lady Gregory. Their intent was to turn away from traditional English plays and fashion a distinctively Irish theater. In 1904, the company moved to a refurbished theater on Abbey Street.

THE GAELIC ATHLETIC ASSOCIATION

The most popular sports in Ireland are Gaelic football and hurling, both distinctively Irish. They are loved for their speed and violence, but just as much because they are Irish, not British.

The preservation of Irish sports has a history going back to 1893, when the Gaelic Athletic Association was formed. A letter by one of the founders, Dr. Thomas Croke, archbishop of Cashel, summed up the association's viewpoint, one that also says much about how the Irish feel about the British. This excerpt is found in *The Course of Irish History*, edited by T. W. Moody and F. X. Martin.

> [Ireland is] importing from England not only her manufactured goods . . . but her games also and her pastimes, to the utter discredit of our own grand national sports and to the sore humiliation of every son and daughter of the old land. . . . And what have we got in their stead? We have got such foreign and fantastic field sports as lawn tennis, polo, croquet, cricket and the like—very excellent I believe, and health-giving exercises in their way, still not racy of the soil but rather alien on the contrary to it. . . . If we continue travelling . . . in the same direction . . . condemning the sports that were practiced by our forefathers . . . and putting on [England's] other effeminate follies as she may recommend, we had better at once, and publicly, abjure our nationality, clap hands at the sight of the Union Jack, and place England's "bloody red" exultantly above the "green."

The Abbey became famous—infamous, some thought—for its realistic portrayal of Irish life. In 1902, Yeats's *Cathleen ni Houlihan* was, for the time, a bold expression of Irish nationalism. The production of John Millington Synge's *The Playboy of the Western World* in 1907 caused a riot in the audience because of its frank look at Irish peasantry.

In addition to Synge and Yeats, many of the greatest playwrights in the history of the English language have come from Ireland—Oliver Goldsmith, William Sheridan, George Bernard Shaw—and the tradition continued with Brendan Behan and Séan O'Casey. In the 1990s such dramatists as Brian Friel (*Dancing at Lughnasa*) and Martin McDonagh (*The Beauty Queen of Leenane*) are keeping Irish drama alive. And although Samuel Beckett lived in Paris and wrote his plays in French, the Irish proudly claim him as one of their own.

William Butler Yeats is just one of Ireland's many literary giants.

Storytelling in Irish culture has been extended to poetry. In addition to Yeats, Ireland has produced such famous poets as Patrick Kavanagh and Austin Clarke. So great is Ireland's fondness for verse that Dublin's rapid transit stations reserve—among all the advertising posters—a display case for poetry. Novelists have been more rare, although James Joyce is perhaps the best ever produced by Ireland or anywhere else, and Bram Stoker's *Dracula* is an enduring favorite.

The Irish love of living can be summed up in a single word. In Irish it is the word *craic*, pronounced "crack." It can be broadly translated as "fun," but it goes far beyond that. It is a way of making the most of what comes one's way, of finding humor in everything and everyone—including one's self. It is a friendliness and hospitality that ensures that, wherever you go in Ireland, you are never a stranger for long.

EPILOGUE
THE HOPE OF PEACE

Peace is much like the exquisite Irish crystal crafted at Waterford—painstakingly difficult to make, so easy to break. Time and again during the three decades of the Troubles, hopes for peace have rested on fragile agreements that have been shattered by a terrorist's bomb. Would the 1998 Good Friday agreement suffer the same fate?

The early signs were doubtful. In July members of the Orange Order massed for a march through the Catholic sections of Drumcree only to be blocked by riot police and British troops. Ten Catholic churches were set afire. At Ballymoney, north of Belfast, a Catholic house was firebombed on July 19. Three brothers, ages ten, nine, and seven, were killed. Even as Protestant leaders condemned the violence, the province braced for reprisals from the IRA. They never came. The peace held.

Then, on Saturday, August 15, a car bomb exploded in the busy market town of Omagh. Twenty-eight people were killed during the explosion, and one man later died of his wounds. More than two hundred were injured, many critically. Among the dead were three generations of a single family—a sixty-five-year-old woman, her pregnant daughter, and her eighteen-month-old granddaughter.

THE REAL IRA

The world recoiled in horror at the single deadliest event in the long, bloody conflict. A splinter group of the IRA calling itself the Real IRA claimed responsibility, but it insisted that it had not meant to kill civilians. If this was intended as an apology, no one accepted it. If the bombing was intended to abort the peace process and create a wider split between Catholic and Protestant, it failed utterly.

Throughout Ireland—north and south—people across the religious and political spectrum were joined in grief and

outrage. In Dundalk, just south of the border, Bernadette Devlin, long a heroine of the Catholic cause, was forced by people shouting "Shame!" and "Murderer!" to close the store she owned with Mickey McKevitt, widely thought to be a leader of the Real IRA. "Dundalk has been known for some time as a republican town, and even an IRA town," said local attorney John Woods. "But, this current IRA crowd, they speak for nobody. The very definite message to these people from their neighbors is, 'Get out of our town.'" [28]

Even the IRA had had enough. It called on the Real IRA to disband, and Sinn Féin's Gerry Adams called for restraint. On September 1 Adams made what was regarded as a momentous statement, saying that "the war is over" and that violence must now be "a thing of the past, over, done with, and gone." [29] No Sinn Féin or IRA leader had ever formally rejected violence, which was long considered a legitimate weapon in the fight for freedom.

In the summer of 1998 a car bomb exploded in Omagh, Northern Ireland, claiming twenty-nine lives. A splinter group of the IRA claimed responsibility.

Sinn Féin president Gerry Adams condemned the violence in Omagh and has vowed to pursue non-violent tactics to achieve peace in Northern Ireland.

BOLD STEPS

Adams had taken a bold step, and now David Trimble, the new Assembly's first minister, did likewise. The Unionist leader invited Adams to a face-to-face meeting, risking the wrath of both Ian Paisley's right-wing party and some elements of his own. Trimble did, however, show some caution, saying there would be no public handshake between the two men.

The meeting took place on September 10 at Stormont—Trimble and Adams, alone, for thirty minutes. If there was no warmth when the meeting was finished, at least there was no animosity, and Trimble even referred to Adams as "Gerry." Both men, however, agreed that much had to be done before peace was achieved. Decommissioning, the giving up of weapons by paramilitary groups on both sides, was sure to be a long, difficult process. Yet the impression—and the hope—was that Adams, Trimble, and all the politicians were conscious of the overwhelming desire of all Ireland for peace.

Peace—the word was to be seen everywhere in Ireland in September 1998. It was sculpted into a flower garden at the posh Beleeck pottery factory in Northern Ireland, was chalked on billboards in Galway, and was colored in crayon by a child and displayed in the window of a Dublin apartment. Tourists in the great cathedrals were still for a moment each noon, joining in prayers for peace.

The Irish felt that, after so many disappointments, the best chance for peace was at hand and that another disappointment might mean that future generations would have to endure more Omaghs. U.S. president Bill Clinton echoed this feeling when he spoke in Omagh in September. "It's your will for peace that has brought your country to this moment of hope," he said. "Don't let it slip away. It will not come again in our lifetimes." [30]

FACTS ABOUT IRELAND

(Asterisk indicates statistics are for Republic of Ireland only)

LAND

Land area: 32,589 square miles (Republic of Ireland, 27,137; Northern Ireland, 5,452)

Lowest point: sea level

Highest point: Carrantuohill (3,414 feet)

*Land use: crops, 13%; pasture, 68%; forests, 5%; other, 14%

Major cities: Dublin (Republic), 1,200,000; Belfast (N.I.), 295,000; Cork (Republic), 173,700; Londonderry (N.I.), 100,500; Limerick (Republic), 76,500

PEOPLE

Total population: 5,129,000 (1997 estimate) (Republic of Ireland, 3,525,000; Northern Ireland, 1,604,000)

Population density: Republic of Ireland, 129 persons per square mile; Northern Ireland, 294 persons per square mile

*Average age at marriage: females, 23; males, 24

*Average years of education: females, 8.8; males, 8.6

*Percentage of people over 25 with some college education: females, 6.5%; males, 9.3%

*Birthrate: 16.1 births/1,000 population (world rank, 134th)

*Infant death rate: 9 per 1,000 births (1985 estimate)

*Number of children per woman: 2.28 (world rank, 127th)

*Occupants per household: 3.7

*Per capita income: $9,950

*Life expectancy: males, 73.24 years; females, 78.89 years

*Religions: Roman Catholic, 95%; Anglican, 3%; other, 2%

ECONOMY

*Gross domestic product: $59.5 billion

*Gross domestic product (per capita): $12,430 (world rank, 22nd)

*Gross national product (per capita): $12,130 (world rank, 23rd)

*Economic composition: agriculture, 8.9%; industry, 38.6%; services, 52.5%

*Unemployment: Republic of Ireland, 12%; Northern Ireland, 11.2%

*Exports: chemicals, computer equipment, industrial machinery, agricultural products; total value, $43.4 billion

*Major export partners: United Kingdom, 26%; United States, 17%; Germany, 14%; France, 9%

*Imports: food, animal feed, petroleum and petroleum products, machinery, textiles and clothing; total value, $32.7 billion

*Major import partners: United Kingdom, 37%; United States, 17%; Germany, 7%; France, 4%

*Government expenditure per capita: $3,392 (world rank, 21st)

*Agricultural production: grains, 2,050,000 tons (world rank, 65th); cattle, 5,637,000 head (37th); horses, 52,000 (65th); sheep, 4,991,000 (43rd)

TRANSPORTATION

*Roadways: 57,433 miles (53,987 miles paved; 3,446 miles unpaved)

*Persons per automobile: 3.8 (world rank, 77th)

NOTES

Introduction: "A Terrible Beauty"

1. Quoted in Patricia Levy, *Culture Shock! Ireland*. Portland, OR: Graphic Arts Center, 1996, p. 22.

Chapter 1: The Land

2. J. H. Andrews, "A Geographer's View of Irish History," in *The Course of Irish History*, eds. T. W. Moody and F. X. Martin. Boulder, CO: Roberts Rinehart, 1994, p. 17.

3. Quoted in Lisa Gerard-Sharp and Tim Perry, *Ireland*. London: Dorling Kindersley, 1995, p. 178.

Chapter 2: The People

4. Quoted in R. F. Foster, ed., *The Oxford History of Ireland*. Oxford, England: Oxford University Press, 1989, p. 9.

5. Quoted in Moody and Martin, *The Course of Irish History*, p. 62.

6. Quoted in Moody and Martin, *The Course of Irish History*, p. 79.

7. Quoted in Moody and Martin, *The Course of Irish History*, p. 105.

8. Quoted in Robert Kee, *The Green Flag*. New York: Delacorte Press, 1972, p. 10.

Chapter 3: England-Ireland; Protestant-Catholic

9. A. R. Orme, *Ireland*. Chicago: Aldine, 1970, p. 23.

10. Quoted in John Ardagh, *Ireland and the Irish*. London: Penguin Books, 1995, p. 21.

11. Adian Clarke, "The Consolidation of Ulster and the Rebellion of 1641," in Moody and Martin, *The Course of Irish History*, p. 203.

12. Quoted in John O'Beirne Ranelagh, *A Short History of Ireland*. Cambridge, England: Cambridge University Press, 1994, p. 70.

CHAPTER 4: THE TROUBLES

13. Quoted in Ranelagh, *A Short History of Ireland*, p. 266.

14. Quoted in Tim Pat Coogan, *The Troubles.* Boulder, CO: Roberts Rinehart, 1996, p. 69.

15. Quoted in Moody and Martin, *The Course of Irish History*, p. 363.

16. Quoted in Coogan, *The Troubles*, p. 384.

17. Quoted in Barry Hildebrand, "The End?" *Time*, April 20, 1998, available from http://www.time.com.

18. Quoted in Barry Hildebrand, "A Big 'Yes' for Peace," *Time*, June 1, 1998, available from http://www.time.com.

19. Quoted in Barry Hildebrand, "The People's Choices," *Time*, July 6, 1998, available from http://www.time.com.

20. Quoted in Kathy Sheridan, "Quiet Hope Instead of Confidence," *Irish Times*, April 13, 1998, available from http://www.irishtimes.ie.

21. Quoted in Hildebrand, "The End?"

CHAPTER 5: SEEING THE AGES OF IRELAND

22. Quoted in H. G. Leask, revised by H. A. Wheeler, *St. Patrick's Rock, Cashel.* Dublin: Stationery Office for National Parks and Monuments, n.d., p. 17.

23. Adrian Tenniswood, *County Fermanagh: Castle Coole, Florence Court, the Crom Estate.* London: Centurion Press, 1998, p. 14.

CHAPTER 6: A PEOPLE IN TRANSITION

24. Quoted in Ardagh, *Ireland and the Irish*, p. 160.

25. Quoted in Ardagh, *Ireland and the Irish*, p. 163.

26. Quoted in Hildebrand, "A Big 'Yes' for Peace."

27. Quoted in Ardagh, *Ireland and the Irish*, p. 213.

EPILOGUE: THE HOPE OF PEACE

28. Quoted in T. R. Reid, "'Get Out of Our Town,'" *Washington Post*, August 20, 1998, available from http://www.washingtonpost.com.

29. Quoted in Deaglán de Bréadún, "Trimble Invites Sinn Fein Leader to Talks," *Irish Times*, September 2, 1998, available from http://www.irishtimes.ie.

30. Quoted in Gene McKenna and Dominic Cunningham, "Reach Out for Peace; Don't Let It Slip Away," *Irish Independent*, September 4, 1998, available from http://www.independent.ie.

CHRONOLOGY

B.C.

ca. 6000
Ireland is settled by Mesolithic people.

ca. 3200
Newgrange passage tomb constructed.

ca. 3000
Neolithic culture begins.

ca. 1800
Bronze Age begins in Ireland.

ca. 500
Celts begin to arrive.

A.D.

431
Pope Celestine commissions Palladius to convert Irish to Christianity.

432 or 459(?)
St. Patrick begins work in Ireland.

548
Clonmacnoise monastery founded by St. Ciaran.

550–750
Golden age of Irish monasticism.

795
Viking invasions begin.

976
Brian Boru becomes king of Munster.

1002
Brian Boru becomes king of united Ireland.

1014
Vikings are defeated by Brian Boru at battle of Clontarf;
Brian is killed.

1169
Anglo-Norman English land at Bannow Bay.

1171
English defeat Irish-Viking army at Castleknock; English
supremacy established.

1174
Irish kings submit to King Henry II of England.

1234
Construction of Dublin Castle begins.

1366
Statutes of Kilkenny forbid English to marry Irish, speak
Gaelic, or wear Irish clothing.

1494
Poynings's Law limits power of Irish Parliament.

1534–1537
"Silken Thomas" Fitzgerald leads revolt against English.

1601
English complete conquest of Ireland with victory at battle
of Kinsale.

1607
"Flight of the earls" to France.

1609
Protestant settlers begin plantation of Ulster.

1641
Irish participate in Ulster revolt.

1649
Oliver Cromwell leads troops through Ireland.

1654
Cromwellian Settlement of Ireland begins.

1690
William III defeats James II at battle of the Boyne.

1691
James II's French allies surrender at Limerick; Protestant Ascendancy begins.

1695–1709
Penal Laws against Catholics are enacted.

1791
Theobald Wolfe Tone founds United Irishmen.

1793
Catholics regain right to vote and hold office, except in Parliament.

1795
Ulster Protestants found Orange Order.

1798
French-aided Irish revolt fails.

1801
Act of Union makes Ireland part of United Kingdom.

1823
Daniel O'Connell forms Catholic Association.

1828
O'Connell is elected to Parliament despite ban on Catholics.

1829
English Parliament lifts all restrictions on Catholics.

1845–1849
Great Famine kills more than 1 million; another million emigrate.

1848
Young Ireland revolt is crushed by British.

1858
Irish Republican Brotherhood ("Fenians") is formed.

1879
"Land War" begins.

1884
Gaelic Athletic Association is founded.

1893
Gaelic League is founded.

1908
Sinn Féin party is founded.

1912
Protestants sign Ulster Covenant vowing to oppose home rule.

1916
British troops put down Easter Rising; subsequent executions solidify Irish in opposition to Britain.

1918
Sinn Féin wins majority of Ireland's seats in Parliament, proclaims Irish republic, and establishes the Dáil Éirann.

1919–1921
Anglo-Irish War.

1921
Anglo-Irish Treaty signed in London; six counties of Northern Ireland vote to remain part of Britain.

1922–1923
Irish fight civil war over treaty with Britain.

1937
Irish constitution is approved.

1949
Republic of Ireland proclaims itself free of all connection with Britain.

1967
Civil rights movement begins in Northern Ireland.

1968
Protest marchers in Londonderry are attacked by police; incident is beginning of "the Troubles."

1972
British troops in Londonderry kill thirteen protest marchers on "Bloody Sunday"; British impose direct rule of Northern Ireland.

1973
Republic of Ireland joins European Union.

1985

Anglo-Irish agreement calls for cooperation of Britain and Republic in seeking solution in Northern Ireland.

1994

IRA calls cease-fire; Sinn Féin president Gerry Adams meets with government officials; President Bill Clinton allows Adams to visit United States.

1995

Adams withdraws from peace talks; IRA ends cease-fire; U.S. president Clinton promises to work for peace in Northern Ireland; George Mitchell is named to chair peace commission.

1997

IRA calls second cease-fire.

1998

(April 10) All parties sign Good Friday agreement; (May 22) voters in north and south overwhelmingly endorse Good Friday agreement; (June 25) first Assembly elected in Northern Ireland; (August 15) car bomb kills twenty-nine people in Omagh.

Suggestions for Further Reading

Sam H. Bell, *The Hollow Ball*. Belfast, Ireland: Blackstaff Press, 1990. Fictional story of a young soccer player set against the backdrop of Belfast in the 1930s.

Maude Casey, *Over the Water*. New York: Puffin Books, 1996. An Irish girl living in England gets a better understanding of her background when she visits relatives in Ireland.

Eileen Dunlop, *Tales of St. Patrick*. New York: Holiday House, 1997. A fictionalized account of the life of the saint largely responsible for the conversion of the Irish to Christianity.

Morgan Llywelyn, *Brian Bóru: Emperor of the Irish*. New York: Tor Books, 1995. An adaptation of Llywelyn's adult novel for younger readers. Fictional account of the life of the first king of all Ireland.

———, *Strongbow: The Story of Richard and Aoife*. New York: Tor Books, 1996. The two characters—the Norman invader and the Irish princess—alternate first-person narratives in this fictionalized biography of the man who began the conquest of Ireland in the 1100s.

Elona Malterre, *The Last Wolf of Ireland*. New York: Clarion Books, 1990. A boy and girl find three wolf cubs and are determined to protect them from landowners who have vowed to kill all wolves in Ireland.

Carolyn Meyer, *Voices of Northern Ireland*. San Diego: Harcourt Brace, 1987. The author interviews people about their experiences growing up during "the Troubles" in Northern Ireland.

Kenneth Morgan, ed., *The Young Oxford History of Britain and Ireland*. New York: Oxford University Press, 1998. An excellent overview of the histories of Britain and Ireland and how they are intertwined.

Don Nardo, *The Irish Potato Famine*. San Diego: Lucent Books, 1990. One in the World Disasters series, this book examines the historical and human factors of the famine that killed more than a million people in Ireland in the 1840s.

Mark O'Sullivan, *Melody for Nora*. Chester Springs, PA: Wolfhound Press, 1997. A fictional story about a fourteen-year-old girl who helps a wounded soldier during the Irish civil war of 1922.

WORKS CONSULTED

Books

John Ardagh, *Ireland and the Irish*. London: Penguin Books, 1995. An insightful look at the Irish based on three years of research in Ireland and hundreds of interviews. Ardagh portrays the Irish as a society trying to adjust to a modern, complex world.

Tim Pat Coogan, *The Troubles*. Boulder, CO: Roberts Rinehart, 1996. A comprehensive account of the Catholic-Protestant struggle in Northern Ireland. All the facts are here, but the author seems biased toward the Catholics.

R. F. Foster, ed., *The Oxford History of Ireland*. Oxford, England: Oxford University Press, 1989. Six essays on different phases of Irish history. The period before 1700, however, is covered much more extensively than later ones.

Lisa Gerard-Sharp and Tim Perry, *Ireland*. London: Dorling Kindersley, 1995. One of the Eyewitness Travel Guide series, this book contains many informative articles on history and culture in addition to descriptions of tourist sites.

Robert Kee, *The Green Flag*. New York: Delacorte Press, 1972. A massive account of Ireland's struggles for freedom from British dominance. This book details the major divisions on the rise of republicanism under Wolfe Tone, O'Connell and the Union, Parnell and home rule, and the Anglo-Irish War of 1919 to 1922.

H. G. Leask, revised by H. A. Wheeler, *St. Patrick's Rock, Cashel*. Dublin: Stationery Office for National Parks and Monuments, n.d. This guidebook has excellent photographs and both historical and archaeological details on all major buildings.

Patricia Levy, *Culture Shock! Ireland*. Portland, OR: Graphic Arts Center, 1996. Levy takes a sprightly look at various aspects of life in Ireland—everything from politics to pub etiquette.

Denis McCarthy, *Dublin Castle: At the Heart of Irish History.* Dublin: PrintStone, 1997. Much more than the usual guidebook, this well-researched volume traces the history of Dublin Castle throughout Celtic, Viking, Norman, and modern times.

T. W. Moody and F. X. Martin, eds., *The Course of Irish History.* Boulder, CO: Roberts Rinehart, 1994. This text offers twenty-three essays on various periods of Irish history by a distinguished collection of scholars. Originally published in 1967, this updated edition contains two new chapters that deal largely with the conflict in Northern Ireland.

Newgrange: A Step Back in Time. Mullingar, Ireland: Midlands-East Tourism, 1998. A very good guidebook to the three passage graves of Newgrange, Knowth, and Down. All the archaeological data are here, plus a healthy dose of legends surrounding the sites.

Marie O'Brien and Conor Cruise O'Brien, *A Concise History of Ireland.* New York: Beekman House, 1972. A good brief history liberally illustrated with drawings and photographs. Its lack of maps is a drawback, however.

A. R. Orme, *Ireland.* Chicago: Aldine, 1970. A comprehensive examination of the geography of Ireland and the role it has played in the island's history.

John O'Beirne Ranelagh, *A Short History of Ireland.* Cambridge, England: Cambridge University Press, 1994. An excellent overview with especially good accounts of Northern Ireland and the Republic of Ireland since the division of 1922.

George Otto Sims, *Exploring the Book of Kells.* Dublin: O'Brien Press, 1988. Intended for children, this book tells in simple language the history of the Book of Kells and how it was made. It contains very good color photographs and black-and-white illustrations.

Adrian Tenniswood, *County Fermanagh: Castle Coole, Florence Court, the Crom Estate.* London: Centurion Press, 1998. An excellent history and architectural description of three Georgian estates in Northern Ireland.

Periodicals

Deaglán de Bréadún, "Trimble Invites Sinn Fein Leader to Talks," *Irish Times*, September 2, 1998.

Barry Hildebrand, "A Big 'Yes' for Peace," *Time*, June 1, 1998.

———, "The End?" *Time*, April 20, 1998.

———, "The People's Choices," *Time*, July 6, 1998.

Gene McKenna and Dominic Cunningham, "Reach Out for Peace; Don't Let It Slip Away," *Irish Independent*, September 4, 1998.

Muintir Acla (*People of Acla*), no. 3, Spring 1996.

T. R. Reid, "'Get Out of Our Town,'" *Washington Post*, August 20, 1998.

Kathy Sheridan, "Quiet Hope Instead of Confidence," *Irish Times*, April 13, 1998.

INDEX

Picture Credits

About the Author

William W. Lace is a native of Fort Worth, Texas. He holds a bachelor's degree from Texas Christian University, a master's from East Texas State University, and a doctorate from the University of North Texas. After working for newspapers in Baytown, Texas, and Fort Worth, he joined the University of Texas at Arlington as sports information director and later became the director of the news service. He is a senior administrator at a community college system in Fort Worth. He and his wife, Laura, live in Arlington and have two children. Lace's other books include biographies of baseball player Nolan Ryan, artist Michelangelo, and statesman Winston Churchill, and histories of the Hundred Years' War and Elizabethan England.